HISTORIC MORNINGSIDE

A

HISTORIC MORNINGSIDE

Lands, Mansions and Celebrities

With
" ANNALS OF THE PARISH "
and some account of
ECCLESIASTICAL MORNINGSIDE

By
WILLIAM MAIR, F.R.S.E.

1947

First Published 1947

MACNIVEN & WALLACE

(John Menzies & Co., Ltd.)

138 Princes Street

Edinburgh, 2

Printed and Bound in Edinburgh by

H. & J. PILLANS & WILSON

1947

PREFATORY NOTE

" ANTIQUITY ! thou wondrous charm, what art thou ?
that, being nothing, art everything !
The mighty future is as nothing, being everything !
the past is everything, being nothing ! "

CHARLES LAMB, *Essays of Elia*, 1823.

THIS historical sketch is based partly on an article contributed by the author on the same subject to the *Book of the Old Edinburgh Club*, and partly on the author's *Centenary History* of Morningside Parish Church. The opportunity has been taken to extend the itinerary to include the Estates in the area to the southern boundary of the city, and to similarly widen the outlook on Ecclesiastical Morningside.

Acknowledgment and thanks are here rendered to many interested friends for suggestions, also for valued assistance and material; to the contributors named in the text, and for constructive criticism.

To the memory of other friends who have helped,
this book is gratefully dedicated.

W. M.

32 BRAID HILLS ROAD,
EDINBURGH, 10.
October 1947.

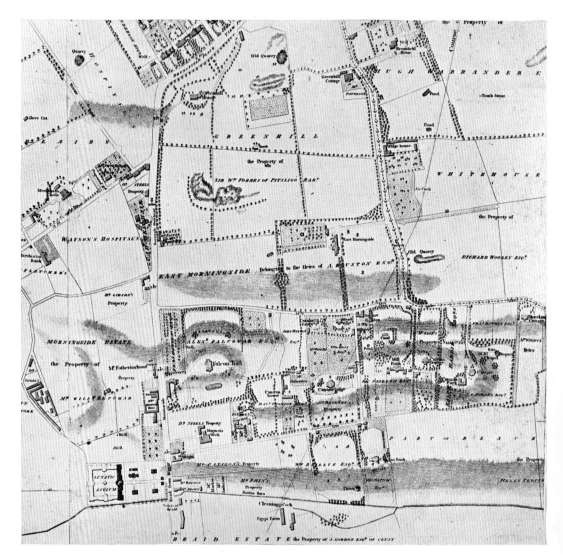

KIRKWOOD'S MAP, 1817 (MORNINGSIDE AREA)

HISTORIC MORNINGSIDE :
LANDS, MANSIONS, AND CELEBRITIES

THE history of this sunward suburb of the city has been well and fully narrated by the late Dr W. Moir Bryce in his exhaustive treatise " The Burgh Muir of Edinburgh, from the Records " (*Book of the Old Edinburgh Club*, vol. x., 1918, the whole of that volume of 278 pages, being devoted to it). The present study is therefore largely an endeavour to record some notes about the more or less famous personalities who have lived in the district or have been connected with it, and about more or less notable locations.

The whole area under consideration, embracing the lands of Greenhill, Burghmuirhead, Easter and Wester Morningside, and Canaan, formed the western part of the Burgh Muir, which in its turn had been part of the ancient forest of Drumselch, gifted to the city by the saintly King David I. of Scotland. It is bounded on the west by the lands of Craiglockhart, Myreside, and Merchiston, and on the east by the estates of Bruntsfield, Whitehouse, Grange, and Blackford. The accompanying reproduction, from Kirkwood's Plan of the City of Edinburgh and its Environs (1817), shows the area dealt with—from Burghmuirhead to the Old Toll at the foot of Morningside Road—and will furnish a comparison with the later development of the district. This was contributed to the *Book of the Old Edinburgh Club*, vol. xxiv., 1942, and is here partly reprinted by permission of the Council and the Editor, Mr Henry M. Paton. The itinerary is now continued from that point to Fairmilehead, a distance of over three miles from Wright's Houses where stood the toll-bar for Morningside (page 38) near Tollcross (Towcroce) where there was no toll. The original Wrychtishousis was a mansion occupied by James Gillespie, the benevolent snuff manufacturer (1717–97) who bequeathed £12,000 to build a hospital, converted in 1870 to an educational foundation, and £2700 to build a school. The house was pulled down in 1800, and the site is now Gillespie Crescent.

Before dealing with the various estates in detail, it may be well to repeat Dr Moir Bryce's identification of them with the portions of the Wester Burgh Muir feued by the Magistrates in the year 1586, departing from their original intention of feuing out the Muir in separate lots each of 3 acres. There were six lots. Lot 1 (14 acres) was absorbed in the sergeantry lands of Bruntsfield, and with it this narrative has no connection, nor with the adjacent Provostry lands of Whitehouse which were not included in David I's gift of the Burgh Muir. The city did not obtain power to feu any part till 1508. Lot 4, consisting of 26 acres, was feued to Andrew Naper (Napier), merchant, and his wife; it became the Estate of *West Morningside*. Lot 6 (feued to Andrew Stevinsoun) contained 18 acres, of which fifteen made up the Estate of *East Morningside*. Lot 5, consisting of 8 acres and two small pieces of ground feued to Thomas Aikenheid, merchant, constituted the original portion of *Greenhill*; and to it were afterwards added Lot 2 (3 acres, 1 rood) feued to Thomas Paterson, and Lot 3 (3 acres, 3 roods) feued to William Rig, with the remaining 3 acres of Lot 6. One of the two small pieces above referred to as part of Greenhill became known later, with other subjects lying to the south, as *Burghmuirhead*. The boundaries of the " common mure " of Edinburgh may be restated as the Loch (now the East and West Meadows) on the north; and the Jordan Burn (then called the Pow Burn) on the south; it was bounded on the east by the present Dalkeith Road and on the west by Blackford Avenue, Kilgraston Road, and the back-greens of Marchmont Road and Marchmont Crescent. The area of Bruntsfield Links is all that now remains of the Muir as an open space.

I

GREENHILL ESTATE

Lot 5 (the original lands of Greenhill) " remained in the possession of the Aikenheads until the year 1636, when it was sold by James Aikenhead to John Livingston. . . ." Thomas Aikenhead, the original feuar, was a skinner (glover) in Edinburgh, and occupied the positions of councillor, bailie, and " dean of gild " in the city. He had at least two sons, Alexander and James. Alexander must have succeeded to the property after his father's death (prior to 1606), and seems to have given to it the name of " the Laird's hill," for under that appellation he disposed of it in 1619 to David Aikenhead, then dean of guild, thereafter provost of Edinburgh, being either unable or unwilling to retain possession. Meanwhile his brother James had died, leaving a son who is styled " Mr James Aikenhead, advocate," and he was served heir in April 1623 to his grandfather Thomas in the subjects under review, having by this time obtained a disposition thereof from the said David Aikenhead (with ratification by Alexander of all right and title that David had from him). It is not stated what relationship the provost bore to Thomas Aikenhead's line, but it was at least a friendly one, which did not end with this transaction; for in later years his grand-daughter Anna, the child of his eldest son, Thomas Aikenhead, commissary of Edinburgh, became the wife of Dr John Livingston of Greenhill, whose father (as narrated in the next paragraph) purchased the estate from the above James Aikenhead in 1636.

8

LANDS, MANSIONS, AND CELEBRITIES

When John Livingston entered into contract with Aikenhead on 2nd July 1636 for the purchase of the estate, he is described as merchant burgess of Edinburgh ; but at his marriage to Elizabeth Rig in April 1626, he is called " apothecary," and he is similarly described in his Testament confirmed 16th October 1649. His wife was a sister of John Rig, advocate, and may also have been related to William Rig, proprietor of Lot 3 which was afterwards added to Greenhill. Livingston's enjoyment of the property did not however last long, for he died in 1645, one of the numerous victims (it is supposed) of the plague which visited the city in that year. It was a virulent epidemic, acutely infectious, complicated with symptoms of a typhus character and pneumonia. At least he was buried within the grounds of his own estate, and in the private garden of a villa in Chamberlain Road may still be seen the tombstone which his widow, Elizabeth Rig, erected over his grave. The walled enclosure is in the form of an unroofed mausoleum, with doorway and pediment above. Over the entrance are carved the initials J L and E R and the date 1645. There is frequent confusion between this stone and one mentioned by Wilson (*Memorials*, i. 213—1891 ed.) as situated near Warrender Park. While in some respects similar there are differences in the initials and shield. There is little doubt that the Warrender stone commemorates a member of the Rig family. The lands of Baglap, or Rigsland, later incorporated in the Bruntsfield estates, belonged in 1645 to Mr John Rig, advocate, whose wife was a Rig of Carberrie, while he himself was of the Aithernie family.

Probably it was in his time that the estate became known as Greenhill, as is hinted in a title of the year 1666. The mansion-house was erected after his death, and was a rambling old house of four storeys. During the period when window tax was imposed it seems to have had thirty-two windows, a few of which were later blocked up. Its appearance at the time of its demolition in 1884 is depicted on the sculptured stone panel (above) designed by Sir G. Washington Browne,

COMMEMORATIVE PLAQUE
From photo by W. Mair.

P.R.S.A., architect of part of the residential property built on the extensive site. This panel may be seen at the corner of Bruntsfield Gardens, opposite Bruntsfield Avenue. The iniquitous window-tax of the eighteenth century was imposed in 1696 and repealed in 1851. It led people to block up their windows, reducing light and air in their houses.

John's widow, Elizabeth Rig, died about 1677. There were two sons of the marriage: the elder son, John Livingston, a doctor of medicine, married (before April 1664) Anna Aikenhead, grand-daughter of David Aikenhead the provost, while she was a minor. When she came of age, in January 1665, she disposed of her half of the lands of Byrecleugh, in Berwickshire, which she had inherited probably from her mother, Anna Home. Dr John was infeft in Greenhill as heir to his father on 19th September 1666, and at the same time in properties then in the possession of John Tweedie. He had however described himself as " of Greenhill " in earlier documents. He was perhaps rather ambitious, or had expended a good deal on the building of his new mansion, for he borrowed considerable sums between 1664 and 1668. By 16th April 1669 he had resigned his lands and house of Greenhill in favour of his brother William. In this connection an interesting document exists showing that the doctor had found difficulty in meeting his commitments, and his brother had to come to his aid and became responsible for his debts. Dr John then betook himself to Stirling, but was forced by further distress at the instance of some creditors to return to Edinburgh and take refuge in the Abbey, " to his great charges and the loss of his calling."

His brother, William Livingston, writer in Edinburgh, married in November 1664, Margaret Cunningham, eldest daughter of George Cunningham, an Edinburgh merchant. They had issue a daughter, Elizabeth, served heir to her mother who was dead before May 1670. On 24th October 1662, he obtained from the Magistrates a charter of the lands of " Ballope " (Baglap) " now called Rigsland," and described himself as " of Rigsland." On 19th September 1666, he took infeftment in other subjects belonging to Rig. He became proprietor also of Greenhill on 16th April 1669 by charter from the Town, on the resignation of his elder brother, as above narrated, and thereafter described himself in several documents as " of Greenhill."

The Livingstons parted with their lands in 1670 to one John Kennedy, apothecary, burgess of Edinburgh ; yet William Livingston is found subscribing a bond in favour of his brother " at Greinhill " on 8th April 1671. The facts are, however, that William mortgaged the estate on 29th September 1668 to Kennedy for the sum of £9080 Scots money, with the manor-place lately erected, and the dovecote in the south yard, and fish pond in the park, etc. So William had obtained possession of the lands before he got his charter from the Magistrates. Kennedy passed on the mortgage to Adam Garden, by disposition dated 3rd August 1672, and when Garden took infeftment on 23rd August 1673, William Livingston was dead. Dr John died in 1675.

By this time Elizabeth Rig, now spouse to Thomas Beg, merchant, conveyed to her son, 3 acres, being the north part of 18 acres in the Wester Burgh Muir bounded by a highway of 24 ells broad on the east (Whitehouse Loan), another road on the south (Grange Loan), a highway of 24 ells broad on the west (Morningside Road), and six fixed stones " between the said part and the common or broad way leading towards the common stane dykes of the lands of William Rig and Thomas Paterson " on the north, all in terms of a Charter by the Magistrates following upon a disposition thereof to Elizabeth Rig in liferent, by Andrew Stevenson, minister at Dunbar, reserving the houses, etc., belonging to him lying on the west side of the highway that leads to Braidsburne (*i.e.*, his property at Burghmuir-head), which Charter was dated 25th November 1657.

Adam Garden (or Gairn) of Greenhill married, in February 1681, Janet Durie, the widow of John Kello, writer in Edinburgh. It was, how-ever, by a former marriage, in March 1668, to Janet Steill, that he had two sons and a daughter, all of whom seem to have died at a comparatively early age. Andrew and John were witnesses to their sister Janet's marriage contract in 1693 with Thomas Fairholm ; but the year 1707 proved a fateful one, for Adam (the father), John, and Janet all passed away in that year, and probably Andrew was also dead, as there is no further mention of him. It happened therefore that the heir to the estate was Adam Fairholm, eldest son of the above marriage.

Thomas Fairholm, husband of Janet Garden, was a merchant in Edin-burgh, became a burgess in September 1724, and later a bailie, besides becoming proprietor of Pilton. He was the only son of Thomas Fairholm, merchant bailie, and Elizabeth Sydserf. By this marriage with Janet Garden he had at least three sons and a daughter. Andrew, the second son, died without issue about 1749 ; Thomas, the third son (a merchant in Edinburgh and made burgess a week after his father), was then served heir to Andrew, along with his sister Janet, wife of Mr David Scott, minister in Edinburgh. (*Fasti Ecclesiæ Scotianæ*, 1, 407. Also *East Lothian Biographies*. (Haddington, 1941.)

The eldest son, Adam, was served heir to his grandfather, Adam Garden, on 19th August 1707, took formal possession of Greenhill in December 1720, and as late as 1764 took sasine of properties in Liberton's Wynd which had belonged to his grandfather from 1658. In 1733 he was served heir in the lands of Lugate, in the parish of Stow, to his uncle John

11

Garden, who had died twenty-six years before. Adam became burgess of Edinburgh in February 1730, by which time he had been twice married : first in January 1720 to Isobel Pringle, daughter of James Pringle of Green-knowe, and, secondly, in July 1729 to her cousin Sophia Pringle, daughter of James Pringle of Torwoodlee. Among the issue of one or other of these marriages were : Thomas Fairholm, merchant, made burgess on 6th April 1757, and George Fairholm, who succeeded to Greenhill after his father's death, which took place at " Greenhill near Edinburgh " on 2nd September 1771. George was also served heir to his father in April 1778 in the lands of Nether Lugate. In 1785 he purchased the lands of Greenknowe, in Ber-wickshire, from James Pringle of Bowland, brother of the above Sophia. He also purchased the lands of St John's Chapel, in the parish of Lauder, and other properties near Melrose, which however he made over to his brother William Fairholm, who is thereafter described as William Fairholm of Chapel, and who married in October 1780, Elizabeth Crompton, daughter of the before-mentioned James Pringle of Bowland.

George, now described as of Greenknowe, having by this time parted with Greenhill, died in " Georges Square, Edinburgh," in the beginning of the year 1800, and was buried in the enclosure at Chamberlain Road, in terms of the privilege reserved to himself and his family when he sold the estate to Thomas Wright in 1790. His brother William died in February 1805, and was succeeded by his eldest son, Adam Fairholm of Chapel. In *Kay's Portraits* (John Kay, 1742–1826, caricaturist) there is a sketch of George, and a note that he and his brother William had long resided in Holland, where they became wealthy bankers, the former also acquiring there an important art collection. They became extensive shareholders in the Bank of Scotland and other financial concerns. The above account of the Fairholms of Greenhill is given in some detail, because there were other contemporary Fairholms in Edinburgh bearing similar Christian names but only distantly, if at all, related.

Wright's trustees sold the lands in 1806 to William Forbes, who in the same year succeeded his father, the great Scottish banker, as 7th Baronet of Pitsligo, Aberdeenshire (cr. 1626). He was author of *Memoirs of a Banking House* (1803), which later became in 1838 the Union Bank of Scotland. This work he dedicated to his son, the 7th Baronet. Sir William Forbes & Co.'s Bank in Parliament Square, then the fashionable business quarter, occupied a court approached by a passage from the Square. Pitsligo was purchased in 1781, having been forfeited by the Jacobite Lord Forbes. (Hence Forbes Road and Pitsligo Road.) The gateway to Greenhill House stood at the junction of Bruntsfield Place and Forbes Road. It was Sir William who forestalled Walter Scott, then a law student, in the affections of the only child and heiress of Sir John Wishart Belsches (afterwards Stuart), Bart., of Fettercairn and Invermay. The estate of Fettercairn came thereby into

THE PARISH CHURCH, 1838
From the Architect's drawing

the Forbes family. The story of this early romance is well known, and is given in Lockhart's *Life of Scott*. Forbes had been a widower for sixteen years at the time of the crisis, 1826–27. In gratitude to him for his generous gesture at the settlement, the bank being among the largest creditors, Scott wrote in his *Journal* that " Forbes behaved as he had ever done, with the generosity of ancient faith and friendship."

The 8th Baronet, Sir John Stuart Forbes (1804–66) of Pitsligo and Fettercairn, who then resided at Greenhill House, presented in 1838 the site of Morningside Parish Church[1] at the corner of what then became Church Lane, later, in 1868, Newbattle Terrace. This name is derived through a marriage connection between the Forbes family and that of the Marquess of Lothian. Thus it comes about that four of the five churches clustered about this ecclesiastical hub of Morningside are built on the lands of Greenhill. There would have been five but Sir John repeatedly refused to grant a site for a Free Church. On the northern corner of Chamberlain Road, western end, stood the Athenæum,[2] formerly the United Presbyterian Church, built 1863, which body sold it and built on the south corner in the Norman style of architecture in 1881. In 1873 Greenhill House was purchased from the trustees of Sir John Stuart Forbes by the Rt. Rev. James R. A. Chinnery-Haldane (1842–1906), Bishop of Argyll and the Isles, who in 1882 disposed of it to a firm of builders (Beattie's). The profit which the Bishop made by the sale of this property was handed by him it is understood, to the Episcopal Church in Scotland. The stone used for the building of Bruntsfield Place and adjoining properties was taken from three quarries opened in the grounds of the old house.

II

EAST MORNINGSIDE ESTATE

The lands of East Morningside lay between what is now Churchhill on the north and Newbattle Terrace on the south, the eastern boundary being Whitehouse Loan. As has been indicated, they consisted of 18 acres

[1] To this day a nominal feu-duty is payable by the Parish Church to the estate, now owned by the 21st Baron Clinton (cr. 1299), C. J. Hepburn-Stuart Forbes-Trefusis, G.C.V.O., son of the 20th Baron and Harriet Williamina, daughter of Sir John Stuart Forbes, 8th Bart., of Pitsligo (later Hepburn-Stuart). The Forbes connection with this district is perpetuated in the name of Clinton Road.

[2] The Athenæum was a concert hall for the district and stood on the site of what is now the fine new Congregational Church at Chamberlain Road corner. Previously the site had been occupied by the first Morningside United Presbyterian Church (1863–81), which was replaced by the present structure on the opposite corner ; the original building was sold to the Athenæum Company for £2000. There are thus four Churches at that location—North Morningside (Church of Scotland) ; Christ Church (Episcopal) ; Congregational ; and Baptist (the latter formerly the Free Church built 1843)—five, if the Parish Church nearby is included.

feued off the Wester Burgh Muir in 1588 to Andrew Stevenson, merchant in Edinburgh, and in the year 1657 his grandson Andrew disposed of 3 acres thereof to the Laird of Greenhill, and sold the remainder to Thomas Beg, merchant. Forty years later Easter Morningside came into the possession of Sir William Menzies of St Germains. He was succeeded in 1723 by his son, Thomas Menzies of Letham and Gledstanes, advocate. He sold the subjects in February 1726 to Gavin Baillie, merchant in Edinburgh, who built the present mansion-house shortly thereafter. Gavin Baillie died in September 1734 and is described as " of Morningside," the earliest occurrence of the name yet found.[1] Later proprietors were successively William Murray, Deputy Receiver of Customs ; his daughter Margaret Murray of Pitkeathly, she married in 1762 William Mercer of Aldie. Her father became proprietor of the lands of Pitkeathly and was a descendant of the Murrays of Ochtertyre. Other proprietors were Alexander M'Millan, W.S., who died in July 1770 ; his cousin Duncan M'Millan, W.S. ; and, in 1786, Alexander Houstoun. Kirkwood's map shows that East Morningside House stood alone at that date in its extensive demesne stretching from Whitehouse Loan to Morningside Road, a distance of three-eighths of a mile, later divided up into lots of two and three or four acres. Here died in 1829, James Ferrier, W.S., who in the late eighteenth century lived at 25 George Street, and was among the first to welcome Burns to Edinburgh. On more than one occasion the poet spent an evening with him. It was to Ferrier's eldest daughter that Burns addressed the lines enclosing the *Elegy on Sir J. H. Blair*. His other daughter, Susan Edmonston Ferrier (1782–1854), wrote charmingly of Scottish society of her day. Sir Walter Scott was a colleague of her father in his office as Principal Clerk of Session, and he thereby knew all the leaders of the literary society of Edinburgh at that date. In this environment, and in this hospitable home, Miss Ferrier's first novel *Marriage* was written. It was published at first anonymously in 1818 and Blackwood paid £150 for it. Encouraged by its success Blackwood gave her £1000 for *The Inheritance*, also written here and published anonymously (1824). *Destiny* was published seven years later. These, from her clever portraiture of Scottish life, were attributed to Scott, by whom her writings were greatly admired. Other admirers of her works were Lord Brougham, Sydney Smith, and Macaulay. From " Morningside House "

---

[1] The origin of the attractive name, Morningside—and what relation it had, if any, to the Lanarkshire village of that name or to Morningside Heights, New York, the location seven miles up-town of Columbia University (its Charter granted by King George II. in 1754, New York State and twelve others being till 1783 a British Colony), which crowns the plateau, and of the vast Cathedral of St John the Divine and the beautiful white marble St Luke's Hospital —it has not been possible to discover. There is a reference in the Town Council Register of 1756 to the farm lands of Easter Morningside.

she wrote (1820),[1] " We are once more settled here and glad I am to find myself out of the smoke and dirt of the town, which always disagrees with me at this season—the air of this place suits me particularly well." Among other letters one is dated " Morningside, 1823." Lockhart describes the delicacy with which she helped Scott (when visiting Abbotsford in 1831) over the gaps in talk caused by his failing memory. A frequent visitor at East Morningside House was her nephew James Frederick Ferrier (1808–64), appointed Professor of Civil Law in the University of Edinburgh in 1842, and from 1845 till his death, Professor of Moral Philosophy at St Andrews —" the last of the metaphysicians " she called him. He married in 1837 his cousin, the eldest daughter of Professor John Wilson, " Christopher North," also of this intellectual coterie. James F. Ferrier published in 1856 the works of his father-in-law (and uncle) in five volumes, including the *Noctes Ambrosianæ*.

Another notable owner of this house in Clinton Road was John Montgomerie Bell, W.S. (1837–1910), who composed many fine tunes and anthems (among them St Giles), and was a member of the Committee which prepared the Scottish Church *Hymnary*. He was the son of A. Montgomerie Bell (1808–66), Professor of Conveyancing at Edinburgh, whose works on that subject are still standard. The old house, with its immensely thick walls and original oak panelling intact and surrounded by its two acres of well-kept gardens, retains all its rural charm. The late Lord Fleming, one of the Senators of the College of Justice, owned the house till his decease in 1945. It is now in the possession of a distinguished medical specialist.

The ivy-covered square dove-cot in the garden has 232 nesting places on the four inside walls. It is exceptional in having the roof sloping to the cold north. Part of a fine avenue of beech trees which led to the house can still be seen in the grounds of Woodcroft, on the south side of Clinton Road.

An interesting relic which stands beside the dove-cot is the venerable trunk of a willow tree grown from a cutting brought from Napoleon's garden at Longwood, St Helena.

Closely adjoining, but with its entrance gate on Whitehouse Loan, is Clinton House, where lived the widow of Lieut.-Gen. James Kerr Ross, who served under Wellington. She built the house in her seventy-first year and lived in it, with all her faculties bright, till her decease in 1909 at 103 years. She remembered Waterloo, and at the age of ninety-one she wrote a military march for the Diamond Jubilee, 1897, which was accepted by Queen Victoria. When at 102 years of age she bought a new grand piano, she replied to an inquiry, " I practise a little every day."

[1] *Susan Edmonston Ferrier, Memoir and Correspondence*, by John A. Doyle (1898).

LANDS, MANSIONS, AND CELEBRITIES

Opposite, on Clinton Road, are three mansions which between them occupy 8 acres of park and garden ground, still unencroached upon, extending to the southern boundary of the old estate at Newbattle Terrace, a remarkable preserve almost in the heart of a city. These lands and those of Clinton House just mentioned are shown on the plan of 1817 as part of East Morningside. The first is Woodcroft, built about 1860 by Lieut.-Col. Sir David Davidson, H.E.I.C.S. (born 1811, at Haddington), of beautiful sandstone quarried within its own grounds. At its elevation of 300 feet it still commands, as he described it, " a view of Blackford, the Braids, and Pentland Hills, stretching one behind the other like the scenery of a stage." [1] A motto over the doorway (deleted by a later owner) was suggested by Jane Welsh Carlyle, *meliora semper cogita* (always think of better things), on account of Col. Davidson's and her own associations with Haddington and taken from an old house there. One of the two others is The Elms, where lived George Wilson, M.D., F.R.S.E. (1818–59), the founder and first director of the Industrial Museum, succeeded by the Royal Scottish Museum in 1861. When he died he had collected 10,350 specimens for " his dear museum " as he called it. His brother was Sir Daniel Wilson (1816–92), author of *Memorials of Edinburgh in the Olden Time*. Both brothers lived at Elm Cottage, as it was called then, each occupying half the house, so named after the magnificent elms on the property. Thirty Newbattle Terrace was the home of Mary Carlyle Aitken, wife of Alexander Carlyle, M.A. (1843–1931) ; she was the companion and amanuensis of her distinguished uncle in his later years. Mr A. Carlyle presented to the National Library of Scotland a valuable gift of manuscripts of the Sage of Chelsea. At Newbattle House, Pitsligo Road, died the Dowager Lady Liston Foulis, eldest daughter of Robert Cadell, partner of Constable, and sole publisher, after 1826, of Scott's works.

III

BOROUGHMUIRHEAD

The dividing line between the estates of Greenhill and Easter Morningside on the east, and properties on the west hereafter to be mentioned, was the road of ancient origin wending its way through the Muir, and known as the " wester hiegait " to distinguish it from what was called the easter road leading to Dalkeith and the Borders. On the west side of this highway are two places to which only passing reference need be made, as they are really outwith the bounds of the present monograph. The first is Montpelier, which at its original feuing in 1767 to Hugh Buchan, writer in

---

[1] *Memorials of a Long Life*, by Lieut.-Col. D. Davidson (Edin. 1890).

Edinburgh, is simply described as four acres of ground in the south-west-most part of the uppermost great park near to the head of Bruntsfield Links, and was for a long time afterwards known as Wright's-houses Park. It is probable that he erected the mansion-house. In 1782 Buchan is described as Chamberlain of the City of Edinburgh, and subscribes a deed at Wright's-houses Park. In 1810 he was succeeded by his son James, physician in H.M. Forces. Thereafter the property passed into the hands of Alexander Henderson, banker in Edinburgh, who disponed it in June 1820 to Robert Scott " now of Montpelier," the subjects being described as " part of the lands of Wright's-houses now called Montpelier with the dwelling-house and offices." The origin of the new name has not so far been traced. It is possible that it may have had some relation to the fact of Saint Roche having been born at Montpellier, (page 34) the mildness of the climate in the hollow having, at times, some resemblance to that in the south of France.

The second is Merchiston Castle, " whilom seat of a race second to none in Scotland for rank and talent—the Napiers." When the illustrious John Napier [1] (1550–1617) was born in the castle, his father, Sir Archibald Napier, was not quite sixteen years of age. His eldest son, the ninth Laird, was master of the Scottish Mint for thirty years. He found workable quantities of gold in the Pentlands " not in vaynes but rather in rocks neere the tops and heights of the mountaynes." All such gold, including that better known from Leadhills (highest village in Scotland), was minted in the Scottish coinage till the Union of the Parliaments in 1707. In 1424 Parliament had granted these sources to the Crown by whom they were leased to experienced " miners." The Scottish Cunzie House was opened in 1574, in Mint Close, High Street. The Mint was finally demolished in 1867 : over the main doorway was a lintel with the letters C.R. II, surmounted by a crown and the inscription " God Save the King," 1675. Some of the instruments used are in the Antiquarian Museum, Queen Street, Edinburgh.

IV

CHURCHHILL

This select neighbourhood was so named when Dr Thomas Chalmers (1780–1847), then Professor of Divinity in the University, built the first house there. He opened Morningside Parish Church (page 13) in 1838, having been largely instrumental in its promotion, there being till then no

---

[1] John Napier died in the Castle, 1617. His famous work on *Logarithms* was printed in Edinburgh, 1614.

place of worship nearer than St Cuthbert's.[1] He had not long been settled at No. 1 Churchhill when the disturbed relations between Church and State culminated in the Disruption of 1843. He founded later the New College of the Free Church, in which he became Principal and Professor of Divinity. He had resigned his chair at the University, while nearly 500 ministers of the Church of Scotland under his leadership gave up their livings, some of them the richest in the country. A bronze tablet on the house reads: " In this house Thomas Chalmers died, 31st May 1847." It was here that he preached for some succeeding Sundays " planted midway up the staircase to a disjoined congregation, scattered over the different rooms, all of whom could hear but not half of whom could see the clergyman."[2] They later formed, with him, the Free Church (now the Baptist Church), built near Colinton Road corner in 1843, having had the use of the Schoolhouse till the new building was ready. Orator, philosopher, and statesman, his statue, erected in 1876 at the intersection of George Street and Castle Street, was executed by Sir John Steell, from whose chisel is also the classic marble bust of this great Scotsman in the Upper Library of the University of Edinburgh.

THOMAS CHALMERS,
D.D., D.C.L., Ll.D.

Just beyond Churchhill, at 24 Greenhill Gardens, lived the above Sir John Steell, R.S.A. (1804–91), Sculptor-Royal for Scotland. His most familiar work is the equestrian statue of the Duke of Wellington in front of the Register House (" the Iron Duke, in bronze by Steell "). " Marvell-

[1] " He took a house at 2 Morningside Place where he remained for about a year and he became so pleased with his then quiet country quarters that he fixed on building his later house which he called Churchhill and to which he returned when finished in 1842 from a house at 7 Inverleith Row; he occupied Churchhill for five years till his sudden death in 1847. Dr Chalmers' temporary residence in 1837–38 at Morningside Place naturally suggested to him, in which he was vigorously assisted by many others, the desirability of an Extension Church being erected there as the whole church-going population of the district, and many beyond, had to travel every Sunday to the Old West Kirk or one of its Chapels of Ease at Gardner's Crescent, Buccleuch Street, or Newington. . . ." From a letter, dated 1891, by Mr David Chalmers, son of the Doctor's brother Charles, who was first Headmaster of Merchiston Castle School. *Courtesy of Mr Daniel Macniven.*

[2] *Memoirs of Dr Chalmers,* by his son-in-law, William Hanna, D.D.

ously life-like " is said to be his statue of Sir Walter Scott enshrined in the Monument, with the favourite stag-hound Maida at his feet. Other public statues by Steell are those of Queen Victoria crowning the façade of the Royal Scottish Academy ; the Albert Memorial, Charlotte Square ; and Allan Ramsay. Another resident of Greenhill Gardens—No. 27—was Henry J. Bell, artist : about a dozen of his Scottish landscapes were hung in the Royal Academy, London, between 1894 and 1899.

Midway between Churchhill and Newbattle Terrace stands the " Bore Stone," erected on a pedestal at the north-west corner of the boundary wall of Morningside Parish Church. It is described and illustrated on page 53 of this book.

This section of Morningside Road was long known as Banner Place, with Banner Villa,[1] Banner Lodge, and Flodden Lodge, names arising from the tradition attached to the Bore Stone, brought into prominence by Sir Walter Scott in his poem *Marmion*. Bank House, formerly Morningside Bank (as indicated on the 1852 Ordnance Survey map), with the conservatory at the head of the steep entrance steps—which with the twelve-foot wall to the street (six feet on the garden side) seems to indicate the embankment on which the house stands—was built in 1790. Here the late Dr Cosmo Gordon Lang, until 1942 Archbishop of Canterbury, and his brother, the Very Rev. Dr Marshall B. Lang, author of *The Seven Ages of an East Lothian Parish*, spent part of their boyhood in the later years of their father's distinguished ministry of Morningside Parish Church, 1868 to 1873, afterwards (1909) the Very Rev. John Marshall Lang, C.V.O., D.D., LL.D., Principal of Aberdeen University. The Archbishop, Lord Lang of Lambeth, wrote to the author in connection with the Centenary of the Church commemorated in 1940 : " I have a vivid memory of Morningside Church, as well as of Bank House, whose garden was a great joy to us children."

V

MORNINGSIDE ESTATE

The lands of Wester Morningside stretched along the western side of the King's highway (Morningside Road), from Dow (Doo) Loan to the Briggs of Braid (page 40), so named from a little bridge which once existed there over the Jordan Burn. A recent writer has described the alteration of name from Dow Loan to Albert Terrace as " a revolting change ! " These lands extended to twenty-six acres, having the lands of Merchiston and Myreside on the west, and embracing the villages of Morningside and

[1] Here lived till her decease in 1913 a gifted artist, Miss Hannah C. Preston Macgoun, R.S.W. Her representations of child life have exquisite charm ; she illustrated Dr John Brown's classics, *Rab and his Friends* and *Pet Marjorie*.

Tipperlinn. They were feued in 1586 to Andrew Napier, merchant in Edinburgh, brother of Sir Archibald Napier of Edenbellie, then " Laird of Merchingstoun." He took infeftment on 7th February 1586–87, but evidently renounced possession after a few months, for on 11th August 1587 the magistrates granted a charter of the same subjects in favour of Alexander Napier, son of Sir Archibald, with remainder to Archibald and William, his brothers. The subjects thereafter came into possession of John Cant of Morton, whose son Ludovick Cant disponed them in 1657 to Thomas Beg, merchant in Edinburgh. He was also laird of St Giles Grange and, his son, Andrew, became laird of Comiston. For further particulars of the family see Mrs Stewart Smith's *The Grange of St Giles*, pages 21–25. For the next one hundred and seven years they were owned by William Menzies and successive proprietors of Easter Morningside mentioned on page 15. In the year 1764 they were acquired by John Orr, tenant in Morningside, surgeon in the 36th Regiment of Foot, and thereafter sold (in 1787) by his son to John Mosman, merchant,[1] whose nephew, Hugh Mosman of Auchtyfardle, in 1789 sold them to Francis Garden of Troup, better known as the benevolent but eccentric Lord Gardenstone (1721–93), one of the senators of the College of Justice. In January 1795 his nephew, also named Francis Garden, disposed of the house and properties to David Deuchar, seal engraver, whose youngest son William succeeded in 1808.

By courtesy of Miss Charlotte Ethel Evans.

MORNINGSIDE HOUSE and, on right,
the SMIDDY (formerly the Free Church School)

[1] John Mosman acquired the lands on 7th June 1787 and died 5th October 1787. He had previously purchased the lands of Canaan. Mr W. Forbes Gray has recorded that Burns' Clarinda, Mrs M'Lehose, was a visitor to his place of Auchtyfardle, in Lanarkshire, and wrote (20th August 1813) of pleasant walks in the vicinity, which summoned up " many a tender recollection," and of much kindness " such as makes one forget the past."

Morningside House, a modest mansion (illustrated), the residence of Lord Gardenstone and later of the Deuchar family, stood on the site now occupied by the branch of the Edinburgh Public Library, the lands reaching down to what is now Millar Crescent. His lordship was wont to ride from here to Parliament Square, preceded by his favourite dog and attended by a Highland laddie who ran alongside barefoot and took charge of the horse when his learned master reached his destination. Depicted in *Kay's Portraits*, where also is to be found the reference to his custom of keeping a live pig in his bedroom to warm his clothes. In 1762 he bought the estate of Johnstone in Kincardineshire, including the then small village of Laurencekirk, which under his enlightened fostering became a thriving town and his resort during the court vacations. Lord Gardenstone regularly partook of the mineral water of St Bernard's Well, Stockbridge, and in 1789 he erected over the well the little Doric Temple, with a dome, designed by Nasmyth, after the Sybil's Temple at Tivoli. In 1884, William Nelson, publisher, placed the statue of Hygeia, executed by Steell, beneath the canopy and presented the well and surroundings to the city.

David Deuchar (1742–1808) was an etcher of distinction. In Williamson's *Edinburgh Directory* of 1790–92 (the first was published in 1773) appears "D. and A. Deuchar, seal engravers to the Prince of Wales (afterwards

HENRY RAEBURN AT 17
(Drawing by Deuchar, 1773)

DAVID DEUCHAR AT 30
(Miniature by Raeburn, 1773)

22

George IV.) opposite the Cross, South Side," and another entry is " James Gilliland, jeweller, Parliament Close." It was Deuchar's practice to visit his jeweller friend and neighbour, whose apprentice in 1773 was Henry Raeburn (1756–1823). The story of his discovery and encouragement of the genius of the young Heriot's foundationer is well known. A miniature portrait of the engraver made at that time by Raeburn and a similar token of esteem in the form of a pen and wash drawing by Deuchar of the boy of seventeen were acquired in 1931 by the National Gallery of Scotland from representatives of the family. Mr Stanley Cursiter, O.B.E., R.S.A., R.S.W., has written these descriptions : " Miniature. Head and shoulders, clean shaven, face slightly to the right, but the eyes look straight out, powdered hair with small curls over the ears, grey coat, buff waistcoat, white neck-cloth and frill, light brownish-grey background." Unsigned, on the back is a label " David Deuchar, Esq., of Morningside, by Sir Henry Raeburn, being the second portrait done by him during the time he was an apprentice with Mr Gilland (*sic*) Jeweller, Parliament Square, Edinburgh. Water-colour on ivory, $2\frac{3}{8}$ in. by $1\frac{7}{8}$ in."

Of the drawing (they are framed together), Mr Cursiter writes : " The head is in profile showing a boy in a three-cornered hat, the wig and queue behind, the frilled shirt and jacket of the period. It is curious to turn from the drawing to the late self-portrait and see how Deuchar caught the character of the features we know so well : the full eyebrows, the straight upper and slightly projecting lower lip. Here we have a valuable cross reference establishing the link between Raeburn and Deuchar at the time, as well as a new portrait of the artist." A great-granddaughter (Miss C. Ethel Evans) possesses a collection of David Deuchar's original etchings [1] and beautiful specimens of his seal engraving and cameos, many in heraldic designs, cut on garnets and other jewel stones. As has been noted, his youngest son succeeded to Morningside House and estate under the unusual terms of David Deuchar's will, whereby they *ascended* from younger sons to elder. John Deuchar (1786–1863) became proprietor on the death of a younger brother George in 1834. He had classrooms in Lothian Street, as an extra Mural School of the University and was a lecturer in popular chemistry both in Edinburgh and Glasgow and the first to lecture to ladies in that subject. (See also page 32.) Ultimately, what then remained of the property came to his fourth son, David Deuchar, F.R.S.E. (1843–1905), who was manager and actuary of the Caledonian Insurance Company. When the old

---

[1] In 1788 Deuchar published *The Dance of Death* in forty-six copperplates from the paintings by Hans Holbein the younger, representing each grade of humanity, from pope to beggar, terrorised by Death. In 1943 there was presented to Edinburgh Public Library, bequeathed by the late Mr Kenneth Sanderson, W.S., a magnificent folio edition, in two volumes, of David Deuchar's etchings.

house was pulled down he built, a little way to the rear on what became Morningside Park, Harlaw House, which he sold in 1881 to Morningside Church for use as a manse. The old garden and one or two grass parks were feued, all the rest being absorbed by what was known as the Asylum. Morningside Place was formerly known as Deuchar Street.

The Edinburgh Mental Hospital, now the Royal Edinburgh Hospital for Nervous and Mental Disorders, had by this time acquired, as will be noted later, almost the whole of the lands of Wester Morningside. Till about 1891 the high stone boundary wall ran from Morningside House to Jordan Burn, its somewhat forbidding wooden gate [1] standing just opposite Jordan Lane. It was the entrance to the East House, which was demolished on the opening of Craig House Hospital, created by the late Sir Thomas Clouston, M.D., LL.D., on what has been described as Edinburgh's finest site. It is now better realised that here is a little township of about 1500, for the most part paying patients, and that occupational therapy in a sympathetic and friendly atmosphere and beautiful surroundings is one of the chief factors in restoring mental health, while the modern practice of psychotherapy has been pioneered in its component Jordanburn Nerve Hospital and Clinic, the first of its kind in this country. The inception of a mental hospital for Edinburgh in the mind of the elder Andrew Duncan, M.D. (1744–1828), successor to James Gregory (page 33) in the University Chair of Medicine, is commemorated in a mural monument erected near the entrance porch to the principal hospital, West House. He was born at St Andrews. On May Day morning in 1827, in his eighty-third year, he ascended Arthur Seat as had been his custom for thirty years. This memorial also embodies a bronze bust (a replica of one in the Academy of Medicine, Paris) of Philippe Pinel (1745–1826), the famous French physician and originator of this enlightened treatment. It was inaugurated on the centenary of his death, and of six portrait medallions in bronze one is to Dr Andrew Duncan, senior. In 1806 a Charter of Incorporation was obtained, and a Government grant of £2000 having been secured (drawn from the forfeited estates fund of the '45), the first building was ready for patients in 1813. On completion of the original scheme in 1840 at a cost of £27,734, it became the Royal Mental Hospital. The original building, known as the East House, not now existing, was erected on six acres of what was the southmost part of the 26 acre estate of Morningside—the distinguishing title of Wester having by this time been dropped. This had been sold by Francis Garden in 1793 and was disponed in 1808 to the Asylum Managers. In 1842 they acquired the farm and village of Myreside (46 acres) and by 1853

---

[1] The gardener's cottage beside Tipperlinn House is the original gate cottage as it stood here on Morningside Brae, giving entrance to the East House.

the remaining portions of the quaint little village of Tipperlinn, all forming the western portion and boundary of what was the Wester Burgh Muir. In 1877 the historic manor house of Old Craig House,[1] with its 61 acres of beautiful wooded land, passed into the possession of the Managers, with its vaulted kitchen then 375 years old. The walls of the older part are in

By courtesy of Professor Sir D. K. Henderson, M.D., F.R.S.E.

OLD CRAIG HOUSE

some places ten feet thick. It is occupied as a sylvan retreat for gentle-women. The lintel of the entrance is inscribed L S C P, Laurence Symson and his wife, Catherine Pringle, who built the house, 1565, and there is an armorial panel, on the later portion, of " Sir James Elphinstoun, 1733." An interesting miscellany, *The Morningside Mirror*, has been issued monthly from the hospital with unfailing regularity for a hundred years, the first number having appeared in 1845, then, as now, in a format of eight octavo pages at a penny, all contributions of articles and poetry having been made from within the institution, where it was printed for fifty years.

A treasured relic in the district is the Old Schoolhouse, on Morningside Road, built in 1823 and since 1895 had been until recently in the possession of the family of the late Mr Cowieson, at the foot of whose garden it stands. It has entered on a new life of beneficence as will be found outlined on page 74. It was the village schoolhouse and sufficed for the local children

---

[1] John Hill Burton, LL.D., lived here 1861 to 1878. He was Historiographer Royal in Scotland : the present holder of that office, the distinguished littérateur, Henry W. Meikle, C.B.E., D.Litt., LL.D., is resident in the South Morningside area.

and others from as far afield as Swanston, Fairmilehead, and Lothianburn : and they had to walk the three or four miles. The hands of the clock stand permanently at twenty minutes to four, the "movement" having been transferred, by consent of the school trustees, to the spire of the parish church opposite, where it did duty till worn out and replaced in 1929, a

Photo by W. Mair.

THE VILLAGE SCHOOL, 1823

life of one hundred years. There is an entry in the church accounts : " to School Fund for clock, including case, £19, 12s. 5d." Former pupils in distant parts of the world held the " wee school " in affectionate remembrance, also Baillie's School, now Gillsland Park School, Spylaw Road. It occupied a villa (now Mr Yerbury's photographic atelier, opposite Churchhill) in what was then Marmion Terrace, so named in the wave of adulation for the tradition mentioned on page 20. One of these pupils became Sir David Yule, Bart. (1858–1928), a merchant prince in Calcutta, who established jute and paper industries there and had large interests in tea estates in Bengal. Another recalled that in 1843, following the Disruption, he was taken away from it and put to the Free Church school (shown in the illustration on page 21). The site and that of the old smiddy are covered by the Branch Public Library (erected 1906). The lane adjoining, where the boys played, and fought, remains as it was then, with its " but-and-ben " cottages. It led to Springvalley House, which is commemorated on what is now Springvalley Gardens and Millar Crescent by a sculptured plaque similar to the one of Greenhill House [1] (page 9). The village doctor was George T. Beilby, M.D., who lived in the house immediately to the south of the old school. His son, born here in 1850, was Sir George T. Beilby, LL.D., F.R.S., a pioneer in physical and industrial chemistry. The East House, mentioned above, and the whole of its surrounding land was purchased by the late Mr James Millar. He and his son, Mr A. Walker Millar, F.S.I., erected thereon the houses in Millar Crescent, Millar Place, that part of Morningside Park, and Morningside Terrace. The Jordan Burn skirted the southern side of the grounds of this property but was later covered over by the lane leaning from Morningside Terrace to Maxwell Street, proceeding thence to between Nile Grove and Jordan Lane. Before the Jordan was covered over by the roadway at Briggs of Braid the boys had jumping competitions from side to side of its banks.

The village of Tipperlinn was included, as has been indicated, in the lands of Wester Morningside. It extended from Dove (Dow) Loan, now Albert Terrace, to the Jordan Burn. Myreside was a humbler location, of which only Myreside Cottage now exists, but Tipperlinn, a cluster of small cottages, had a reputation for sunshine and its share of the " best people " from Edinburgh among the summer visitors. The houses had an outside stair, or forestair (such as may still be seen in the Lawnmarket of Edinburgh), and were mostly occupied by weavers whose operatives lived in small thatched cottages adjoining and worked hand-looms in their own homes. Linen damask was woven in floral patterns—one large table-cloth, a specimen of the work of these bygone artists of the looms, with the date 1754 woven in, is in the possession of a descendant, resident in Tipperlinn Road, of one of the master weavers. Another popular product of these looms, also a damask, was the homely " dambrod " pattern in blue and white, or pink and white squares. When Dr Thomas Chalmers joined the Kirk-Session of Morningside Parish Church, Boroughmuirhead, Merchiston, and Tipperlinn became his district for visitation as an Elder. An important chemical industry was founded here in 1770, that of oil of vitriol or sulphuric acid manufacture, then coming into industrial use, by Dr Thomas Steel, surgeon. With Thomas Gladstanes [2] of Leith he formed a company

---

[1] James Grant, author of *Old and New Edinburgh*, lived in Springvalley House.

[2] Thomas Gladstanes was the grandfather of the Victorian Prime Minister. The late Sir James Steel, Bart., Lord Provost of Edinburgh (1900-03), developed a large part of the area under consideration. The schoolboys in 1840 regarded the chemical factory as the " black works." It was later transferred to Glasgow and ultimately absorbed in Imperial Chemical Industries.

as Steel, Gladstanes and Company. Dr Steel also feued in 1797 three acres on the other side of Morningside Road, in Canaan (Now Steel's Place), where he erected works for the manufacture of magnesia, which was beginning to be required in large quantity in Edinburgh and throughout Scotland as a constituent of Dr Gregory's Powder (page 33).[1] By 1853, as has been stated, the Asylum had acquired the remaining feus from the last of the weavers, Henry and George Murray, but not that of the "big house," Viewfield. In the garden the draw-well is still in existence which was the principal water supply of the village. Tipperlinn House, close by, built on part of the site of the old village, is the residence of the Physician Superintendent of the Hospital. In the garden in front of the house is a curious stone, one foot high, with a semi-circular head and the date 1660. It is believed to be one of several in Scotland to commemorate the Restoration of the monarchy, following Cromwell's Dictatorship. The grounds of George Watson's College closely adjoin.

VI

CANAAN

The remaining, and by far the largest, portion of the lands within the immediate Morningside area is that known by the name of Canaan. The estate eventually enclosed an area of 65 acres. It may be best to define the area comprised in the land of Canaan, and to answer if possible the question which invariably arises as to how the district came by these Biblical names, so well known. In the *Report of the Common Good of the City of Edinburgh* [2] it is stated : " The lands of Canaan are bounded on the west by Morningside Road, on the east by the property of Morelands, Blackford Park, and Blackford Brae, on the north by Newbattle Terrace and Grange Loan, on the south by the back gardens of houses in Nile Grove." That represents an area five-eighths of a mile wide by 400 yards deep. Moir Bryce says : " That portion of the lands of Braid forming the southern boundary of those of Canaan was known as Little Egypt in the year 1585, and there can be no question that during the Covenanting period it was the means of introducing the name of Canaan. The first time these lands appear under this designation is, so far as known, the year 1661." Goshen, Hebron, Salem, Eden, and Zion Mount are still definite locations and the quiet country atmosphere yet lingers among the leafy avenues and sylvan byways. Nile Grove was named later in continuance of the tradition.

[1] Its use became universal on its admission to the *Pharmacopœia Edinburgensis* of 1839 and its inclusion in the *British Pharmacopœia* of 1885 and since.

[2] By Sir Thomas Hunter, Town Clerk, and Mr Robert Paton, City Chamberlain, 1905.

LANDS, MANSIONS, AND CELEBRITIES

Falcon Hall was perhaps the most imposing of the many large mansions situated within the lands of Canaan. Extending to 18 acres between Newbattle Terrace and Canaan Lane the boundary wall of the estate to Morningside Road was broken only by the entrance lodge and gates, outstanding in brown and gold, which stood almost opposite the old school. The pillars

By courtesy of Mr John Bartholomew, M.C., F.R.G.S., F.R.S.E.

FALCON HALL

of the gateway were each surmounted by a falcon finely carved in stone. They remained here till 1894, the house itself remaining among its fine elm trees till 1909 when it was demolished to make way for tenement property and, later, very modern residential flats. The gates were re-erected at a property in Corstorphine and ultimately became the entrance to the Scottish Zoological Park. The mansion was built in 1780 by Lord Provost William Coulter, a stocking weaver in Edinburgh, who became the head of a large hosiery establishment in the High Street, " a plain, somewhat illiterate person, he was proud alike of the office he held and of his commission as Captain of the Edinburgh Volunteers." After two years of office as Provost he died in 1810 and was honoured with a public funeral, conducted, as a critic said, " with a parade and show that was gratefully overdone." [1] It

[1] *The Lord Provosts of Edinburgh*, 1296-1932, by Sir Thomas B. Whitson, LL.D., and Miss Marguerite Wood, M.A., Ph.D., 1932.

was Alexander Falconar, of the Honourable East India Company's Civil Service, who, about 1815, added the fine façade, calling the house Falcon Hall as a play on his own name, and the heroic statues, one of Nelson, the other of Wellington, on either side of the doorway. He otherwise greatly embellished the house, and its removal was much regretted in the district. When the house was demolished in 1909 the façade and pediment were re-erected at the Edinburgh Geographical Institute, Newington. Falcon Hall had been the residence for some time previously of the eminent geographer, Mr John G. Bartholomew, LL.D., F.R.G.S., who founded the Royal Scottish Geographical Society in 1884. His son, Mr John Bartholomew, the present Cartographer to the King in Scotland, recalls that, as a boy of eleven, he specially admired one room of the house, a perfect oval, painted by an Italian artist, and representing the wide sweep of the Bay of Naples. Each of the twelve pillars illustrated is a monolith of Craigleith stone, and the entrance hall of the building in Newington preserves also the fine gallery and its ornamental bronze balustrade. Mr Falconar died in 1847 (a square monument stands in the west division of Greyfriars), and he was succeeded in the ownership of the house and lands by his son-in-law, Henry Craigie, W.S. A triple memorial stained-glass window (illustrated) in Morningside Parish Church was erected by his widow in 1867, artist un-known. The estate, with the mansion-house, was purchased in 1889 by the Merchant Company of Edinburgh, for investment and feuing, for £33,000, being £8000 above the upset price, from the trustees of Mrs Craigie and her four sisters. There was spirited bidding at Dowell's, one gentleman having his eye on the acquisition of the ground for a racecourse. The southern boundary wall still stands intact on Canaan Lane. The villagers of Morning-side were always greatly impressed by and long remembered Mr Falconar's large yellow state carriage, with his five handsome daughters and two footmen, as it rumbled out of the big gates.

One of the most eminent of the residents in Canaan was Professor James Syme (1799–1870), who bought the extensive demesne of Millbank with its gardens, meadows, and glass-houses in 1842. Here he lived and here he spent the evening of his days. His greater son-in-law Joseph, Baron Lister (1827–1912), and his Quaker successor later in the Professorship,

> " Of faultless patience, and unyielding will,
> beautiful gentleness and splendid skill," [1]

who was married to Miss Agnes Syme in the drawing-room here on 24th April 1856, recorded that Syme loved to repair in the evenings to his

[1] " The Chief," *A Book of Verses* by William Ernest Henley, 1888, surgical patient of Lister at the old Edinburgh Royal Infirmary.

Photo by Mr William D. Leask.

MEMORIAL TO HENRY CRAIGIE OF FALCON HALL
IN MORNINGSIDE PARISH CHURCH

(1) " An hungered and ye gave me meat."

(2) " Thirsty and ye gave me drink."

(3) " A stranger and ye took me in."

(4) " Naked and ye clothed me."

(5) " Sick and ye visited me."

(6) " In prison and ye came unto me."

Matthew XXV., verses 35 *and* 36.

The six corporal works of mercy ; believed to be portraits of Henry Craigie, W.S.

31

country house, " beautiful Millbank, with its flowers, its matchless orchids and heaths and azaleas and grapes and peaches." In the course of early chemical experiments with crude rubber (conducted in the cellar of the druggist's shop in Lothian Street occupied by John Deuchar, afterwards lecturer in chemistry), Syme discovered its solubility in naphtha, distilled from coal tar, on which he contributed a note to *Annals of Philosophy*, 5th March 1818. He did not patent the discovery, which was developed by Charles Macintosh of Glasgow, immortalised in the waterproof garment bearing his name. Mr Syme, writing from Millbank in 1847, thus expressed his complacency in missing a fortune which the ethics of his profession would have practically precluded his accepting : " For my own part, I gained little credit and no profit by the discovery, except the confidence which results from struggling with a difficulty, and encouragement in endeavouring to accomplish other objects of utility."—(*Memorials of James Syme*, by Robert Paterson, M.D. (1874).) Thomas Carlyle was a guest at Millbank when he came north to deliver his address as Lord Rector of the University in 1866, and Charles Dickens in 1869, on the occasion of one of his visits to Edinburgh when he gave readings from his works at the Philosophical Institution, consulted Syme for a lameness in his left foot. The house (built 1804) has now been replaced by a hospital pavilion in which an engraved tablet commemorates the above circumstance of the marriage. This and two other houses, Canaan Park and Canaan House, and their grounds, covering in all an area of thirty-one acres, now constitute the ideal site of the Astley-Ainslie Institution opened in 1923 for convalescent treatment of patients from the Royal Infirmary of Edinburgh, the two latter mansion-houses having been preserved. Canaan Park was at one time occupied by Charles Hay Forbes, third son of Sir William Forbes, seventh Baronet, and brother of Sir John Stuart Forbes.

Perhaps the most famous of the residents in Canaan was the learned James Gregory (1753–1821), Professor of Medicine in the University, the leading consultant in Edinburgh and indeed in Scotland till his death at sixty-eight, to whom belonged Canaan Lodge and its pleasant grounds of five acres, still unspoilt, " a sufficient distance from Edinburgh to be in the real country." [1] He purchased the house and grounds from John Paterson, architect, in 1814. " The Gregorian physic," wrote Professor Christison, was " free blood-letting, the cold affusion, tartar emetic, and the famous mixture which bears his name." Born at Aberdeen, his mother was a daughter of the thirteenth Lord Forbes. That is why his portrait by Raeburn and his extensive medical library (he was the best Latin scholar of his day) were bequeathed to Fyvie Castle, the library being later presented by Sir

[1] *The Academic Gregories* (Famous Scots Series), by Agnes Grainger Stewart, 1901.

Ian Forbes Leith, Bart., to Aberdeen University. His son, Duncan Farqu-harson Gregory (1813–44), a lecturer in mathematics and chemistry at Cambridge, died at Canaan Lodge. He closed the record of this remarkable family, by fourteen of whose members no fewer than twenty-four University Chairs were held between 1638 and 1844. The house (built 1800) was

By courtesy of Messrs Oliver & Boyd, Ltd.
Professor JAMES GREGORY, M.D.
(Portrait by Raeburn)

occupied by John Gregory,[1] advocate, eldest son of Dr Gregory, and his mother till 1863, and by his sister Georgina until her death (at London) on 25th June 1877. It was rebuilt in 1907, and the last proprietor was the late Thomas G. Nasmyth, M.D., of the Scottish Board of Health, who died in 1937. Other notable proprietors had been Macdonell of Glengarry, the Earl of Fife, and Sir William Keith Murray of Ochtertyre.

[1] Known in his day for his collection of birds. The location in the garden of his aviary and eagle's cage may be seen in the Ordnance Survey Map of 1852. His famous pair of golden eagles was presented by him to the old Zoological Garden at Broughton.

C   33

Before proceeding to enumerate some of the more distinguished Canaanites in art and letters, reference should be made to a remarkable collection of sculptured stones, evidently of some architectural importance, which lay for many years in a yard attached to Bloomsberry House (formerly a laundry) at the corner of Canaan Lane and Grange Loan. They were believed to have been removed to this place many years ago from the grounds of St Roque, a mansion a little to the east, and a legend grew up around them that they were the remains of the chapel erected by the Town Council on the Burgh Muir between 1501 and 1504 and dedicated to St Roque (Roche, born at Montpellier, 1295), whose intercessions were sought by the many victims of the oft-recurring plague. The properties at that corner, including the yard, have now been practically all acquired by the Astley-Ainslie Institution and the interesting monumental relics have been added to the appointments of the gardens there. They are richly carved and decorated with tracery and emblematical figures.[1] Reference to Dr Moir Bryce's reproduction of an engraving of 1789 from Grose's *Antiquities* shows the old chapel to have been of very unpretentious architecture, and the conclusion has been arrived at that they may have come from the fifteenth-century Trinity College Church, taken down in 1848 to make room for the Waverley Station. " It was acclaimed the finest specimen of mediæval architecture in Edinburgh, Holyrood alone excepted." [2] The carefully numbered stones lay on the south side of the Calton Hill for a quarter of a century and what remained of them were in 1872 built into a " reconstruction " at Trinity College–Moray Knox Church, Jeffrey Street, overlooking their original site. There, on some of the stones may still be seen the numbers painted on. Although the actual location of the little sanctuary of St Roche on the Muir is in doubt, it is certain that Canaan Lane was the way to it. It is thus still a *via sacra* to a beneficent ministry of healing.

Literary associations with the district and especially with Canaan are very numerous and of some importance. James Wilson, F.R.S.E. (1795–1856), the naturalist brother of " Christopher North " (1785–1854), married and settled at Woodville, Canaan Lane, in 1824, devoting himself to scientific and literary pursuits. Besides his *Voyage Round the Coasts of Scotland*, illustrated with drawings by his fellow voyager, Sir Thomas Dick Lauder, Bart., he was the author of *Illustrations of Zoology*, 1826, in nine quarto volumes. He furnished all the articles on natural history for the seventh edition of the *Encyclopædia Britannica*, all written here at Woodville. He declined in 1854 the Chair of Natural History in Edinburgh University.

[1] Illustrated in *Sculptured Stones of Edinburgh*, by John Geddie (*Book of the Old Edinburgh Club*, iii. 203–5).

[2] *Historic Edinburgh Churches*, by W. Forbes Gray, F.R.S.E. (1940).

His biographer, Rev. James Hamilton, F.L.S., wrote : " It would be difficult to find a more charming retreat than, in Mr Wilson's possession, Woodville became. In his domain of two acres, snugly ensconced amidst the groves of Morningside, he caught the whole sunshine of the winter noon, forgetful of biting blasts and easterly fogs." [1] This was reflected in *Chronicles of a Garden, Its Pets and Its Pleasures* (London, 1864), written by his niece, Henrietta Wilson, daughter of another brother, Andrew. She took charge of the house after the death of her aunt and lived here till 1863. She greatly resembled her uncle and shared his attachment to plants and animals. A frequent summer tenant was the Rev. Archibald Alison, LL.B., (1757–1839), who had been invited in 1800 by Sir William Forbes and the vestry of the Episcopal Chapel in the Cowgate to become Rector there, later at St Paul's, York Place. He was famous in that philosophical age for

By courtesy of Col. John Cunningham, C.I.E., M.D., F.R.S.E.

MILLBANK, CANAAN LANE

his *Essays on the Nature and Principles of Taste*, the effect produced on the imagination by objects of sublimity and beauty, first published in 1790. His wife was the eldest daughter of a near neighbour, Professor James Gregory. Another visitor to the secluded suburb was Thomas Campbell, the poet (1777–1844), author of *Ye Mariners of England* and *Pleasures of Hope*. He was the guest of Mr Alison. He planted a tree in the garden in August 1837, the reports of whose progress took him back to Woodville, " so full of feeling and information." The tree has not survived. Campbell wrote his greatest poem *The Pleasures of Hope* in Edinburgh at the age of twenty. Dr Gregory took favourable notice of it on its publication, much to the advantage of poor Thomas Campbell. In this still delightful pleasance lived

[1] This may give some clue to the origin of the name—the sunny south side at morning and noon ; " syde " or " side " means district. It has been suggested that it may refer to the side of the city facing the morning sun—the morning side.

Sir James A. Russell, M.D., LL.D., F.R.S.E. (1846–1918), former Lord Provost of Edinburgh and a noted educationist. He married a daughter of James Wilson and succeeded to Woodville. Professor Sir D'Arcy W. Thompson, F.R.S., D.C.L. (Oxon.), St Andrews, recalls that when he was a student at Edinburgh, Russell was chief demonstrator in anatomy to the then Professor, D. J. Cunningham, LL.D., D.C.L., F.R.S., whose son, Col. John Cunningham, C.I.E., M.D., F.R.S.E., presides over the Astley-Ainslie Institution on the Millbank Estate closely adjoining Woodville. Cunningham's *Text-Book of Anatomy* is still the standard work, seventh edition 1937, the first having been published in 1902. At Moreland Cottage, now Morelands, about a quarter of a mile to the east, lived Charles Maclaren, F.R.S.E., F.G.S. (1782–1866), co-founder in 1817 with William and John Ritchie, and first editor, of the *Scotsman*. He edited for Archibald Constable in 1820 the sixth edition of the *Encyclopædia Britannica*. A distinguished geologist and President of the Edinburgh Geological Society, he promoted the preservation of a relic of glacial erosion, an ice-dressed rock surface about fifty feet square at Blackford Hill.

SAM BOUGH, R.S.A., 1879
(*From an Etching by Robert Anderson*)

Of the artists, Sam Bough, R.S.A. (1822–79), is the most notable as a personality. He lived on the bank of the Jordan Burn, in what was then called Jordan Bank (now Jordan Lane and re-numbered). He bought in 1866 two houses semi-detached, the other being Jordan Bank Villa, from D. R. Hay, who was architect to Queen Victoria for the interior restoration of Holyrood Palace. A great Scottish landscape painter, Bough is remembered by several of the older residents as a real Bohemian, a large-hearted man generous to a fault. " In contradistinction to the mode adopted by the Puritans he thought to re-christen the place Gomorrah." [1] By contrast, engravings of six of his paintings were published by Blackie (1873) as " authentic views of important Bible localities after Van de Velde and earlier artists." Such was his versatility that he painted an inn sign (still in

[1] *Sam Bough, R.S.A., His Life and Works*, by Sydney Gilpin (1905).

perfect preservation) for the " Volunteers' Rest," as it was then called, which is still familiar in the locality, near where the Old Toll stood. It was so named because the Edinburgh Volunteers held great shooting competitions in the field adjoining, entering by what is now Hermitage Drive. It was the most stirring day of the year in Old Morningside and great crowds flocked out from the city on the summer afternoons. The shooting butts were built on the side of Blackford Hill. Another subject-painter who resided in Canaan Lane was Robert M'Gregor, R.S.A. (1848–1922). A studio built for him at what is now No. 76 still stands.

George Meikle Kemp (1795–1844), architect of the Scott Monument, wrote to his brother Thomas, who was a master of works, from Bloomsberry Cottage, Canaan, 19th May 1838 : " I am quite satisfied with the change I have made from Stockbridge to the land of Canaan ; we have more accommodation for the same rent, a very pleasant little garden enclosed with a high wall, well stocked with flowers and fruit trees—and *very few taxes.*" [1] The details of his life and the tragedy of his death at forty-nine years, when nearing the zenith of his fame and prosperity, are well known. On a dark night and in a dense fog, 6th March 1844, returning to his home at Morningside from the office, on the bank of the Union Canal, of the contractor for the building of the monument, he was drowned, having missed the crossing at Fountainbridge. He was accorded a public funeral, on 22nd March 1844, from his home at 1 Jordan Bank, and a monument was erected in St Cuthbert's Churchyard at the public expense.

There may be noted, set in the stone wall opposite the entrance to Woodburn, Canaan Lane—for many years a Sanatorium and now a Nurses' Home of the Edinburgh Royal Infirmary—two flat stones of about a foot square, incised with the numerals 5 and 7 respectively. The same may be seen in Whitehouse Loan. These, according to Kirkwood's map of 1817, indicate the straight diagonal line of the first Edinburgh public water supply (1681)—" Course of Main Pipe from Bonaly Ponds and Comiston "—to the reservoir on the Castle Hill.

The old village of Morningside lay between Churchhill and the old Toll-house (page 39). Having now noted some of the great and less great among those who have lived in the area, it remains to visualise something of the more ordinary residenters. Truly it was a " Sweet Auburn," and is

---

[1] *George Meikle Kemp*, by his brother-in-law, Thomas Bonnar, F.S.A.Scot. (1892). It is possible to clear up a little confusion which has arisen in regard to his addresses in Canaan. Bloomsberry Cottage is, as in 1838, at the corner of Canaan Lane and Grange Loan. According to the Directory of 1841–42, he had removed to Parkside Street, St Leonard's, overlooking Salisbury Crags, where he loved to sketch. Finally, the entry in that of 1843–44 is " G. M. Kemp, architect, 1 Jordan Lane," practically on Morningside Road, this cottage being replaced by residential property about eighty-five years ago.

so described by a gracious and gentle lady, now in her eighty-ninth year, her health good and her memory unimpaired, who remembers it as a rural paradise, the home of contentment and serenity. On either side of the main highway were the orchards and gardens of the country mansions, and beyond that the farm lands now laid out in streets and attractive terraces. Fringing other parts were the humble whitewashed cottages overtopped by glorious trees. Within living memory the old folks who had been born and brought up in them were loath to leave them, almost until the roof was taken off by the impatient speculative builders of the rows of tall tenements. Some of these comfortable red-tiled " but-and-ben " dwellings still exist, a little way off the beaten track. While between 1790 and 1830 the New Town was evolving on a more or less prescribed basis of town planning, Morningside just grew into an exceptionally dignified residential district. The finely wooded estates were being parcelled out in lots of from five to two acres, many of them, as has been noted, still intact. Others have been entirely superseded by the " flat " system of building, after the manner of the Old Town, whereby a dozen families may enjoy the amenities of suburban residence in the space formerly occupied by one. With the coming of the railway in 1884 and the opening of the Morningside Road Suburban Station, a much greater development of the area commenced.

VII

THE OLD TOLL

At the grass parterre alongside the Braid Church, Nile Grove, almost unique in its octagonal form, the work of Sir George Washington Browne, P.R.S.A., stood the old Toll-house. It does not appear on the 1817 map, nor on the first Ordnance Survey map of the district (1852). On 20th January in that year at a meeting of the Commissioners of Supply and Road Trustees for Midlothian a memorial was submitted, signed by 120 families in Morningside, in regard to the levying of tolls for the district at Wright's Houses, near Tollcross. This had long been felt to be an injustice, restricting improvement and obstructing free intercourse with other parts of the city. It was complained that " we unfortunates of Morningside cannot even visit a friend in Gilmore Place without incurring this exaction," while there was a check-bar at Viewforth, " to catch such as may come by way of Fountainbridge," and another at Grange Loan. Sir John Stuart Forbes, Bart., of Greenhill, supported the petition on the ground that " those who went in by omnibus to their business in the city in the morning and returned in the afternoon, had each to pay twopence extra for toll ; they had to pay one shilling additional on every railway parcel delivered beyond the toll at

Wright's Houses ; their coals were also charged proportionately higher, and so likewise every other article—the parties making the charge, in allocating the price of the toll, in most cases imposing besides a large margin for their own benefit."

Sir James Forrest of Comiston, Bart. (1780–1860), page 48, noted at the meeting that reference had been made to the length of time the toll-

THE OLD TOLL-HOUSE
as it stood at the foot of Morningside Road

bar at Wright's Houses had existed ; it was said to have been there for fifty or sixty years. " Be it so," said Sir James, " but let it be remembered that there was no Morningside at that time at all." He was of opinion that if the toll-bars were removed beyond the city it would lead to houses being built at Morningside and other suburban districts for those who were content to occupy flats in the city, and the houses vacated by these parties would suffer from serious diminution in rents. He thought, however, that they should give effect to the memorial from the residents of Morningside ; and the toll-bar was soon thereafter erected at the then county boundary (1861) at Jordan Burn, where it did duty for thirty years, until the abolition of road tolls throughout Scotland in 1883. *Five years later*, at the instance of Sir John Skelton (page 44), the toll-house was removed and re-erected, stone by stone, as the entrance lodge to his residence, the Hermitage of Braid. On a lintel at the back of the house may still be seen the number

" 259 " which it carried here at the foot of Morningside Road. This door, now built up, was used by the payees, and a wheel in the bay window operated the toll-gate.[1] The low stone wall here, its flat top worn hollow with the " tackety " shoes of generations of schoolboys, figures in the writings of James Laing Waugh (1868–1928), novelist and essayist. He was a clever portrayer of the manners and dialect of Scottish life. In his *Robbie Doo* (1912) and other humorous sketches, and in lectures, he infused into them an element of warm and kindly sympathy, of himself in fact. In his business in George Street he was associated with the grandson of M'Crie, the biographer of John Knox.

" Our Scottish Jordan " as Sir Thomas Dick Lauder (1784–1848) styled it in his delightfully facetious book *Scottish Rivers*, rises in Craighouse Hill and meanders by Nile Grove for about a mile eastwards, partly underground, emerging alongside Blackford Hill Suburban Railway Station, where, in the hollow nestles what remains of Blackford House. Here resided a dear old lady, Miss Memie Trotter, last of a branch of that family. Sir Thomas Dick Lauder was a neighbour at Grange House and a frequent guest. She loved to bathe every day in the Jordan as it passed through her garden, as it does still, on its way to join the Braid Burn at Peffermill, changing its name meanwhile to the Pow Burn,[2] both ultimately reaching the sea at Portobello as the Figgate Burn. The course of the Braid Burn from its source in the Pentlands to this meeting point has been traced on page 47. To the right of the Briggs of Braid a path led to Plewlands Farm, where the Rev. Robert Morehead, D.D., at one time Dean of Edinburgh, wrote in 1823 that he was enamoured of the place : " a most beautiful summer residence near Braid. There is a great deal of poetry scattered about me if I could catch it : the poetry of life is the only poetry worth preserving." He was a cousin of Lord Jeffrey, editor of the *Edinburgh Review*. A large part of the lands here now form a Garden of Rest. Here are interred Alexander Carlyle, M.A., nephew of the Sage of Chelsea, and his wife, Mary Carlyle Aitken (page 17) ; Dr Alexander Mitchell, M.A., Ph.D., historian of Braid Church ; James Logie Robertson, " Hugh Haliburton," poet and essayist ; Alexander W. Mair, M.A., Professor of Greek, Edinburgh University ; William Cowan, President of the Old Edinburgh Club, who bequeathed to the City Library a valuable collection of books and literary relics relating to Edinburgh ; John D. Comrie, M.D., University Lecturer in the History of Medicine ; Alexander John Travers Allan,

---

[1] In 1871 a three-horse bus lumbered between Morningside toll and the east end of Princes Street ; but it did not pay, although the fare was only 6d., passengers to this remote region were so few. Later the trace-horses for the trams (single track) were " parked " by the wall, which still stands, opposite the back of Maxwell Street.

[2] In 1497 it was known throughout its entire length as the Pow Burn.

amateur golf champion of the year 1897, commemorated by his golfing friends ; John H. Romanes, W.S., a historian of George Square ; and " Cummy," Alison Cunningham, the " dear old nurse " of R.L.S.

> " My second mother, my first wife,
> The angel of my infant life."
>
> *Child's Garden of Verses* (1885).

There was then no Comiston Road ; Egypt Avenue led to the farm of that name ; it was just where Nile Grove intersects Woodburn Terrace. In 1799 Mrs Archibald Fletcher, wife of an Edinburgh advocate, was the first to extol the mild and salubrious air of the south side : " seeming to require change of air, we repaired with our children to a very inexpensive cottage in the Morningside district, to the south of Edinburgh, called Egypt." These climatic conditions may have inspired the erection of the Hydropathic, a seven or eight-storey building which stood at the head of Morningside Drive. It became a boy's college. Ultimately it was demolished and the stones used for the building of Morningside Grove.

And beyond the toll—its immediate vicinity as in 1883 is pictured in the illustration on page 66. On the right of the little iron church erected in the open field where the high buildings at the junction of Braid Road and Comiston Road now stand, the latter is seen in its beginnings. Four years earlier R. L. S. had written in *Edinburgh : Picturesque Notes :*—" Just beyond the old toll-house at the foot of Morningside Road the chisels are tinkling on a new row of houses. The builders have at length adventured beyond the toll which had held them in respect so long, and proceed to career in these fresh pastures like a herd of colts turned loose."

VIII

BRAID ESTATE

As will be seen from the map (page 6) the Jordan Burn was the natural boundary of the Braid Estate, as indeed it was then of the city and county. The city boundary was later extended to the foot of the Pentlands, and, later still, to Hillend and the Lothian Burn, when that public park was presented to the city in 1924. Former proprietors were the Henrys, Fairlies, Dicks, and Browns. The name of Braid first appears in that of Sir Henry de Brade, Sheriff of Edinburgh in the time of David I., and for nearly 200 years the estate remained in his family.

Sir William Dick of Braid, also then of the Grange of St Giles, was Lord Provost of Edinburgh in 1638–39 and a zealous Covenanter. He became owner of the Braid estate in 1631 by purchase from Sir Robert Fairlie. It extended to 412 acres and was divided into Upper and Lower Braid,

Braid Hills, Blackford, Plewlands, Greenbank, and Egypt. Dick was reputed to be then worth £226,000 Scots—equal to about two million sterling to-day—from successful trading in the Baltic and Mediterranean. As the result of fines by Cromwell and loans of money to the Scottish estates and Kings, which were not repaid, he came to poverty and died in London, aged seventy-five, in 1665.

Charles Gordon of Cluny bought the estate in 1771 and built the present mansion in 1785, " from the predilection of the beauty and situation." He died in 1814 and was succeeded by Colonel John Gordon in 1858—all as set out on the monumental tablets in the imposing family vaults in St Cuthbert's churchyard. His son, John Gordon of Cluny, died in 1878, and his widow married, in 1880, Sir Reginald Cathcart, captain in the Coldstream Guards. Their heirs were Mr and Mrs Linzee-Gordon of Cluny Castle, Aberdeenshire, who owned, in addition to the Braid estate, the lands of Midmar and others in Banffshire and Nairnshire. On Mrs Linzee-Gordon's decease in 1943 the properties were vested in the Trustees of the Cluny estates. Under their enlightened management the amenities have been preserved and maintained of this extensive area, extending for nearly a mile from Nile Grove to what is called " the Ride " on the Braid Hills.

THE HERMITAGE OF BRAID

From an engraving published Edinburgh, 1796

There was no house between the Old Toll and the gate of the Hermitage of Braid but pastures green, waving corn, and hedges of sweet-scented hawthorn (it is of the family of *Rosaceæ*), all the way up the old Braid Road, to Fairmilehead. The picturesque demesne known for two centuries as the Hermitage is now the property of the citizens through the munificence of a Morningside resident, Mr John M'Dougal, who presented at the same time, in 1938, a sundial in the form of an astrolabe and ancillary sphere, beautifully wrought in bronze by Messrs Henshaw and set on a stone pedestal. The extent of this wonderful amenity, practically within the city, is forty-five acres, and the vegetation of the deep and narrow wooded valley between Braid and Blackford, is luxurious and beautiful in the extreme, all in an orderly scheme of afforestation, planted in two periods, the newer at least 150 years ago and the older 200 to 250 years, in elm, plane, oak, beech, and lime, some of the trees being 250 feet high, casting a cathedral-like shade which, in places, the sun never penetrates. Ferns and mosses and festoons of ivy clothe the steep banks of the ravine to the top. The Braid Burn sings its way through almost a mile of pleasant paths and under rustic bridges, affording truly Arcadian enchantment. Together with the Braid Hills and the Braidburn Valley, closely adjoining, this southern suburb is well favoured.

Some distance to the north of the entrance gate just mentioned, on the old Braid Road, took place what has long been known as the Braid Road Robbery. It is necessary to make only a passing reference to the story and to correct some erroneous statements that have for long been repeated in accounts of this happening, among them that of the genial Miss Margaret Warrender in her *Walks near Edinburgh*. Even R. L. S. in *Picturesque Notes*, referring to the " crow-haunted gibbet " and the stones in the centre of the roadway which may still be seen marking the position where it stood (opposite 66 Braid Road), says that " people of a willing fancy were persuaded, and sought to persuade others, that the stones were never dry. And no wonder, they would add, as the two men who expiated their crime here had only stolen fourpence between them." From a reference to the report of the trial in the *Edinburgh Courant* of 22nd December 1814, it appears that they had assaulted their victim—David Loch, a Biggar carrier, who was bringing a horse to Edinburgh—almost to extinction, taking, as he himself deponed, " four one pound notes, twenty shillings in silver, a two-penny loaf of bread, and a spleuchan, or leather tobacco pouch." The Lord Justice Clerk, the Hon. David Boyle, was determined to put down highway robbery, and apparently considered that the two accused, other offences having been taken into consideration, would, in the famous dictum of Lord Braxfield, quoted by Lockhart, be " nane the waur o' a hangin'—*not* at the ordinary place (at the Tolbooth) but on the spot where you assaulted David Loch, or as near as possible to that spot, and on 25th January 1815." It only remains to add that the *Courant* reported that " we never on any occasion witnessed so great a crowd, who had walked in the snow the three miles from the High Street. The men, both about fifty years of age, spent twenty minutes on the scaffold in their devotions." It was the last execution in Scotland for highway robbery.

On the north and sunny bank of the dell described on page 43 stands the well-built, rectangular, ivy-covered dovecote, in the walled vegetable garden attached to the mansionhouse. It probably belongs to the period of an earlier house, of which there are some traces, supposed to have been known at one time as the Castle of Braid. The dovecote is 35 feet wide by 18 feet broad and is " boxed for doos " to the number of 1965, well-preserved nesting-places of red sandstone. The roof sloping to the sun is ornamented by an elegant stone urn at each corner, and one in the centre. As an unfailing source of pigeon-pie the birds were a usual perquisite of their owners and were maintained at little expense through their depredations on the neighbouring lairds and the poor farmers on whose crops the greedy pigeons fed.

Literary associations circle round the name of Sir John Skelton (1831–97), Scottish essayist and historical writer, who lived for many years here in the Hermitage. He was Chairman of the Local Government Board for Scotland, and wrote under the pen-name of " Shirley," largely in *Blackwood's Magazine*. He published a great defence of Mary, Queen of Scots ; his essays were published under the title of *The Table-Talk of Shirley* and in them he enshrined much of the literary circle he gathered round him at the Hermitage of Braid—Froude, the historian ; Robert Browning ; Dante Gabriel Rossetti ; Thackeray and, among scientists, Huxley and Tyndall.

In recent years the late Professor Charles G. Barkla, F.R.S., of the Chair of Natural Philosophy, University of Edinburgh, Nobel Prizeman in Physics, 1917, resided here. The house, which belongs to the city, is now in the occupation of Mr John T. Jeffrey, A.H.R.H.S., Superintendent of Parks to Edinburgh Corporation, having been gifted to the city at the same time as the " beautiful glen," so described by J. Anthony Froude when writing to Skelton.

A remarkable discovery was made by Mr Robert Waterston and recorded by him in his paper on *Early Paper-Making near Edinburgh* in the *Book of the Old Edinburgh Club*, vol. xxv., 1945, of the existence of a small paper-mill in the valley of the Braid Burn. A mysterious mill-stone has for long lain in the water on the north side about 300 yards upstream from the mansionhouse. Mention of corn mills had appeared in the old charters but a Deed of 1695 revealed the unexpected fact that a " peaper miln " had existed then. This was followed up by the accidental discovery of several old papers at H.M. Register House, showing mill-name water-marks, one of which is reproduced by permission of Mr Waterston.

WATER-MARK on a Deed dated 17th March 1703

A photographic View Indicator was erected on the Braid Hills in 1936 at a point 525 feet above sea-level from which the twenty-five mile panorama may be viewed. The well-known features of the classic outline—towers,

Photo by W. Mair.

VIEW INDICATOR ON THE BRAID HILLS, LOOKING NORTH

45

spires, monuments, and the seven hills surrounding the city—are indicated and named. In the distant landscape the characteristic profile of Ben Lomond may be readily distinguished on a clear day at a distance of 58 miles, with striking views of the Firth and the Fife Hills. It is represented on the plate which will be found at the end of this book, reproduced on one-third scale.

The splendid mile long boulevard between Morningside and Liberton was laid out when the city acquired by purchase in 1889 from the Braid estate, at a cost of £11,000, " the furzy hills of Braid," much of the way cut out of the solid rock. It is now known as Braid Hills Drive, and opposite a point where it becomes Liberton Drive is the Scottish National Observatory. It occupies the eastern shoulder of Blackford Hill (500 ft.), annexed by the City in 1884, the acquisition consisting of 98 acres of hill and dale. The Astronomer Royal is also Professor of Astronomy in the University. On the same extensive site are the King's Buildings of Edinburgh University, where are housed the Departments of Chemistry, Geology, Zoology, and Animal Genetics.

Just past the old steading is the farm-house of Upper Braid where the " fair Burnett," Elizabeth, of Robert Burns' elegy, sought restoration to health in the congenial climate of Morningside and the pine-laden air of the Hermitage, with the ewe and goat's milk whey which was esteemed as a cure for her consumption. She was exquisitely beautiful, the daughter of the eccentric Lord Monboddo, and she died here on 17th June 1790 at the age of twenty-five.

IX

GREENBANK

Andrew Brown, styled as " of Greenbank, Wester Plewlands," purchased on 9th May 1719, forty acres of land between those of Whitehouse and St Roque's Chapel. These subjects were merged, in 1760, with the lands of Blackford, Greenbank, and Over Plewlands as part of the general estate of Mortonhall.

The happy designation of the locality is not uncommon : there is another Greenbank (Gallowgreen) in the St Leonard's district. In 1937 there was added to the amenities of the district, already described, the Braidburn Valley, purchased by the city for the nominal sum of £2000 from Mortonhall estate. It was at once laid out as a public park and Open-Air Theatre, the latter capable of seating an audience of 2500. A thousand children have appeared in various parts of the summer programmes of Morris and other dances and gymnastic displays. Full-scale theatrical performances have been given successfully, the Braid Burn forming an orchestral " pit " between the stage and the auditorium of tiered seats cut out of the grassy slope. An accompanying achievement of landscape gardening, all by Mr Jeffrey, is the floral surround taking the form of a crown in commemoration of the Royal Coronation of 1937. The sparkling jingle of the burn, on its way from Bonaly (also the property of the city

THE LAST THATCHED COTTAGE
(Now Greenbank Drive: the ancient hawthorn bush still exists)

by purchase) in the Pentlands, through the Hermitage and Duddingston to the sea at Portobello, the greenery of the surroundings with the background of towering hills make this as fine an amphitheatre as may be found within the bounds of any modern city. In 1935 four hundred cherry trees were planted by five thousand Guides, Rangers, and Brownies of the City of Edinburgh in honour of the Silver Jubilee of H.M. King George V. Overlooking all is the Braid Hills Hotel, built 1887 (Mrs Gladstone Walker), 500 feet above sea level, which commands uninterrupted views of the city and surrounding country, the river, and the shores of the " Kingdom of Fife."

X

COMISTON ESTATE

At the Greenbank entrance to the Braidburn Valley there stand the two classic stone pillars of the gateway to Comiston House, erected here when the city acquired this land for a public park in 1937. They stood on Comiston Road, near the junction of Comiston Road and the Old Braid Road. At this point (opposite Mortonhall Golf Clubhouse) may be seen the Buckstone, set high in the wall of a private house, Allermuir, where lived J. Cuthbert Hadden (1816–1914), musician and author of a *Life of Haydn*, and other composers. Tradition asserts that it was on this stone that the Lairds of Penicuik stood when giving three blasts on the horn as Royalty passed to the hunt, thus securing tenure of their property in terms of an ancient reddendo in their charter (" free for a blast "), also that the buck-hounds would be unchained here. Comiston House is now occupied as the Pentland Hills Hotel and it retains the fine walled garden. The mansion was built in 1815 by Mr James Forrest, father of Sir James Forrest, Bart., Lord Provost 1837–43, whose name is preserved in that of Forrest Road and, remembered in the well-known contretemps which occurred when Queen Victoria visited Edinburgh in 1842. Her Majesty had arrived at Granton in the Royal George yacht earlier than had been arranged and there was consequently no Provost to present the keys of the city, or Magistrates to receive her.

An earlier name for the estate was Colmanstoun and former lairds were John Fairlie in 1610 and Andrew Creich and his wife, Margaret Dick. A relic remains of a previous castle of Comiston in an old, ivy-covered, round tower dovecote, with about one hundred and sixty nest-holes. From springs on Comiston estate, as is well known, was brought in 1676, when Charles II. was king, the sanction of the Scottish Parliament having been obtained, Edinburgh's first water supply by gravitation, one of the earliest examples of a publicly introduced water supply. Previously many of the larger houses had pumps and draw-wells in their own grounds, as may be seen in the map of 1817, that at Tipperlinn, for example, supplying practically the whole village. The water was led from Comiston, about five miles distant, in a leaden pipe of 3-in. diameter, to a reservoir on the Castle Hill, still existing beside the Outlook Tower and, distributed chiefly from public wells, two or three of which may still be seen, to male and female water-caddies, who brought their stoups and pitchers for their daily supply. Now there are two filtering stations, one at Fairmilehead, which takes care of three and a half million gallons daily, conveyed by an aqueduct thirty-eight miles long from Talla and other reservoirs.

Much of the land here containing the springs, contiguous with the Braidburn Valley, belongs to the city. The Comiston supply is being discontinued on account of the encroachment of housing on the collecting areas and consequent risk of bacterial contamination. There are several, each enclosed in a neat stone building (the interior of the principal one is illustrated) and the water is led from each spring to a collecting cistern, each named and having a leaden figure representing the animal or bird from which it takes its name—the Hare, the Swan, the Tod (fox), and others, here illustrated.

By courtesy of Mr John Bowman, formerly Water Engineer to Edinburgh Corporation.

INTERIOR OF COMISTON WATER HOUSE
showing Hare, Fox, Swan, and Peewit Spring Pipes
Constructed 1676

There is much more of interest in this neighbourhood which can only be dealt with briefly. Swanston Cottage, an early home of Robert Louis Stevenson, to which his father and mother repaired for twelve successive summers (1869–80), with its Queen Anne and rose gardens, is now the home of Mr John Bowman, M.Inst.C.E., F.R.S.E., an ardent collector of Stevensoniana.

The house and the R.L.S. relics are not now open to the public, the latter having been transferred to the Museum at 8 Howard Place, maintained by the R. L. Stevenson Club. Swanston is perhaps the smallest hamlet in Scotland. The latterly few pupils in its miniature school now go to town by bus. There is a farm, no shop, no post-office, and the population has declined in the last twenty years from fifty to about thirty. Although so near the city it is still full of peaceful rural charm and redolent of memories of " the lad that is gone." Several thatched cottages remain.

MILESTONE AT HUNTER'S TRYST

5

miles from the
General Post Office
EDINBURGH
Erected to regulate
the Post-Horse duties
payable
by Hackney Coaches
1824

Emerging from the farm-road below Swanston and about quarter of a mile west of Fairmilehead, where there was a toll (although only two miles from the one at the foot of Morningside Road), four roads meeting here, on the northern side of the road to Colinton is the Caiy Stone, a fine monolith of red sandstone roughly rectangular in shape. It faces almost due east and west and is 9 ft. 3 in. high, with, it is believed, an equal depth in the ground. On the eastern face is a curved row of six small hollows which have been recorded as ancient cup marks.[1] It has also been known as the Camus Stone and the Kel Stane (Battle stone). A little way beyond is a milestone, five miles from Edinburgh, which records that it was set here to regulate the Post Horse duties. Here, on Oxgangs Road is Hunter's Tryst, now a farm, which was an inn until 1862, and had literary associations with Sir Walter Scott, " Christopher North," and the Ettrick Shepherd, and, nearer Colinton on the Redford Road, not far away from " Scotland's Aldershot," is the Covenanter's Monument (1666), a composite column of four pillars conjoined which formed part of the façade of the Old Royal Infirmary (1738) designed by William Adam, architect, father of two distinguished sons, Robert and James, the former of whom designed the plan of Edinburgh University in South Bridge (1789).

[1] *Ancient and Historical Monuments of Scotland* (Midlothian) 1929.

XI

MORTONHALL ESTATE

Reaching Fairmilehead cross-roads (four road ends) and turning to the left by Frogston Road West, is the pleasing little new church of the new Parish of Fairmilehead, built to the designs of Mr Leslie Grahame Thomson, R.S.A., F.R.I.B.A. It was disjoined from Liberton and Colinton and erected into a Parish, 1942. Here also is the Princess Margaret Rose Hospital for Children (Orthopædic) with, behind it, rising to a height of 680 ft., Galachlaw (probably Gallows Law), " betwixt Braids Craigs and the Pentland Hills," where Cromwell and his army of 16,000 men encamped in 1650 before the battle of Dunbar. There will in due course arise, near here, a new military hospital which will bring the hospital population of this southern section of the city, from the cluster of these beneficent institutions at Comiston and Craiglockhart to this point, approaching in all a total of about 8000 patients, from all parts of Scotland.

Fairmilehead is another place-name the origin of which it is difficult to trace. It may refer to the fact that it is equidistant from Hillend and from the " breezy Braids," in Scots parlance a " fair mile " on either side of the summit of the hill. A little over half a mile farther on are the gates of the extensive wooded policies of Mortonhall with its avenues of stately beech, elm, and other trees, extending beyond Kaimes to Liberton. The estate is owned by Captain H. R. Trotter of Mortonhall and Charterhall, Berwickshire, who succeeded his father in 1945, Colonel Algernon R. Trotter, M.V.O., D.S.O., and who thus continues the long and glorious military record of the Trotter family. The St Clairs of Roslin held this property, along with nearby Morton House in the early fourteenth century, in the reign of James III., but since 1641, when it was purchased by the first John Trotter, a successful and benevolent Edinburgh merchant, it has remained in the possession of the Trotter family. The mansionhouse, which was built in 1769, standing on the site of an older structure, and the gardens have a delightful southern exposure, being on a gentle slope. It contains many articles of furnishings which are of priceless value. Stretches of tapestry representing the story of Perseus and Andromeda are exquisitely pretty and are in perfect condition. The house is surrounded by groups of striking centenarian trees, including magnificent sycamores, many widespreading yews, copper beeches, wild-cherry, cedars of Lebanon, and fine old Scotch firs. One of the yew trees has flourished for at least five centuries. A selection of two thousand volumes from the library, sold in London in 1947 realised £7387, among them a copy of John Napier's work on *Logarithms* at £92 (page 18). Morton is believed to have been a Roman town : many coins of that period and cinerary urns have been found in the course of excavations here and at Cramond, where the Romans had a great station and seaport.

The lands of Morton adjoining are also the property of the Trotter family. It was the dower house (usually bestowed on a widow or dowager)

SWANSTON AND THE " T " WOOD *By courtesy of "The Scotsman."*

and it was for long occupied by the historian, John Hill Burton (page 25), who died here in 1881. The carriage-way enters the grounds at a point opposite the hospital.

One other object of local interest is the " T " wood on the White Hill, just above Swanston, under the scarred face of Caerketton (1500 ft.) and a prominent feature of the landscape visible from all over the area. It was planted two hundred years ago by the then laird of Mortonhall, as a memorial to a scion of the house who fell in battle, and takes the form of a cross.

Few cities can have within their area, properties such as this just described, which extends for five miles between north and south—from and including Greenbank to the county boundary at Lothianburn— all well developed on enlightened lines. In some public instances the Superiority is maintained by a clause in the charters of a feu-duty of " a penny if asked." Two private golf courses are situated within the policies, Mortonhall and Lothianburn, and these together with the undulating and diversified Braids public course nearby (one mile east to west by half mile north to south) completes a worthy locus of the game first played by pre-scriptive right of the citizens on Bruntsfield Links in the fifteenth century, still a free course for juvenile devotees and for older generations of players.

LANDS, MANSIONS, AND CELEBRITIES

THE BORE STONE

" Haud fast by the Past "

Photo by W. Mair.

The Bore Stone
In which the Royal Standard was last pitched for
the muster of the Scottish Army on the Borough
Muir before the Battle of Flodden
1513
It long lay in the adjoining field, was then built
into the wall near this spot and finally placed here
by Sir John Stuart Forbes of Pitsligo, Bart.
1852

Highest and midmost, was descried
The royal banner, floating wide;
The Staff, a pine tree strong and straight;
Pitched deeply in a massive stone
Which still in memory is shown,
Yet bent beneath the standard's weight.
Marmion.

This well-known landmark, fixed to the western boundary wall of the Parish Church, epitomises for us something of the history of the spacious Borough Muir gifted to the city by King David I. of Scotland in the twelfth century. He founded the Abbey of Holyrood in 1128, and those of Kelso, Melrose, Jedburgh, and Newbattle, all of which he endowed liberally out of the Crown lands. The conveyance by the city to the Parish Church of St Giles' of part of the ancient forest of Drumselch, included Morningside and the adjacent " village of Tipperlyn."

Perhaps Sir Walter in 1808 helped to weave and perpetuate more tradition round it than later historians would confirm, but the greatest authority on the Boroughmuir, the late Dr W. Moir Bryce, who lived in the locality (Blackford Road), was not disposed seriously to question it.[1]

In the course however of a further masterly historical analysis of the subject by Mr Henry M. Paton, formerly of the Register House, and recorded in the *Book of the Old Edinburgh Club*, vol. xxiv., pages 108–125, he has come to the conclusion that the tradition of the Standard cannot be supported—although for a long period of years and in innumerable books it has been repeated—that it held the Royal Standard at the muster for Flodden in 1513, but he acquits Sir Walter of unduly perpetuating the poetical romance by quoting his Note to

---

[1] *Book of the Old Edinburgh Club*, vol. x. (1918).

Marmion, that " the Royal Standard is *traditionally* said to have been displayed from the Hare Stane " (otherwise the Bore Stone). Perhaps that may be a sufficient conclusion and reservation for us at this late day. The iron tablet bearing the above legend has withstood well nigh a hundred winters without undue erosion and may now perhaps be reprieved.

One relic of tragic Flodden regarding which no doubt exists is the " blue blanket," the pennon of the Earl Marshal, which was carried on that occasion by John Skirving of Plewland Hill, near Edinburgh ; it is now preserved in the Advocates' Library. He was captured at Flodden by the English but managed to conceal the flag round his person.

ECCLESIASTICAL MORNINGSIDE

CHURCH OF SCOTLAND

SCOTTISH EPISCOPAL

BAPTIST

CONGREGATIONAL

ROMAN CATHOLIC

THE BRETHREN

AN ANCIENT CEREMONIAL OFFICE

In 1946 and again in 1947 the Lord High Commissioner to the General Assembly and Supreme Court of the Church of Scotland was a Morningside resident—Rt. Hon. George Mathers, D.L., M.P. for Linlithgowshire, appointed a Privy Councillor in the latter year,—who, with Mrs Mathers, carried out with distinction the duties of this high office, representing the Crown.

A PULPIT IMPASSE

When the pulpit in the Parish Church formerly stood in the central aisle, a Reverend Divine who later became a distinguished Moderator of the General Assembly was on one occasion taking part in a special service along with the late Rev. James M'Gregor, D.D. The occasion was rendered humorously memorable by reason of the Minister of St Cuthbert's ascending the narrow stair, which only admitted the passage of one, while the other was in occupation. The latter retired to the pulpit, hoping that his colleague would give him a free passage, but to his horror and to the congregation's amusement he again proceeded to ascend, resulting in the same contretemps. It may seem incredible but the same performance was repeated a third time, whereupon the invader was finally driven back, to the exasperation of all beholders.

SOME "ANNALS OF THE PARISH"

The Reverend FRANK WOOD

With the inauguration in 1940 of a new and promising pastorate, Morningside Parish Church entered upon its second century in the same spirit of high endeavour as is reflected in these pages, a long and unbroken tradition.

Appointed Assistant in August 1928 to St Andrew's, George Street, Edinburgh, a notable tribute to his scholastic distinction, the Rev. Mr

Portrait by Edward R. Yerbury, F.R.P.S.
1940
Rev. FRANK WOOD, M.A., B.D.

Wood's first charge was at Gilmerton, Edinburgh, to which he was ordained on 6th December 1929. Translated to Kilbarchan West, in the Presbytery of Paisley, on 20th September 1934, his six years' successful ministry there was followed by his recall to his native city of Edinburgh and appointment to Morningside.

He served as a Lieutenant in the 9th Bn. Highlanders, the Royal Scots ("Dandy Ninth") in France and Belgium in 1918 and in the Army of Occupation in 1919. In 1945 he saw service with the Church of Scotland Huts, stationed in Orkney.

HISTORIC MORNINGSIDE :

NOTES ON FORMER MINISTERS

Dr John Marshall Lang was presented in 1872 by Queen Victoria to the famous and historic charge (1595) of the Barony Parish, Glasgow. Soon thereafter he raised £28,000 for building the new Barony Church. Dr Malcolm C. Taylor (page 64) was Secretary to Edinburgh University Court, 1893–1916. A very fine portrait of him by Fiddes Watt, R.S.A., hangs in the University Court Room, presented in 1917. Dr Smeaton was the first Minister, and became Professor in the Free Church College, Aberdeen, later in the New College, Edinburgh, in 1857. Dr Addis was Minister till the schism in 1843 when the Free Church was built, now the Morningside Baptist Church, succeeded by what is now Morningside High. Dr M'Adam Muir, following upon his Ministry of Morningside, was Minister of the First Charge and High Kirk, Glasgow, the venerable Cathedral of St Mungo, founded 1238. He was later Lecturer in Pastoral Theology at Edinburgh and St Andrews Universities, appointed a Chaplain to the King in 1910 and, in the same year, Moderator of the General Assembly, when he published his *Seventh Jubilee of the General Assembly*. He was also author of *The Church of Scotland : A Sketch of its History*. Dr Fisher was translated and admitted as Minister of St Cuthbert's, Edinburgh, on 6th May 1914. He had been appointed a Chaplain to the King in 1913 and was from 1911 to 1914, Edinburgh University Lecturer on Pastoral Theology, and on Apologetics (1913 to 1916). Editor of *Life and Work* from 1902, he was author of *The Four Gospels* (1899), *The Beatitudes* (1912), and other religious books of popular appeal.

FORMER MINISTERS OF THE CHARGE

1839–1841
Rev. GEORGE SMEATON, D.D.

1841–1843
Rev. THOMAS ADDIS, D.D.

1844–1864.   Rev. ROBERT MACGOUN, M.A.
1864–1868.   Rev. ANDREW GRAY, D.D.
1897–1900.   Rev. EBENEZER B. SPEIRS, D.D.

1873–1880
Rev. Professor MALCOLM C. TAYLOR,
D.D., LL.D.

1880–1897
The Very Rev. PEARSON M'ADAM MUIR,
D.D.

The Very Rev.
JOHN MARSHALL LANG,
C.V.O., D.D., LL.D.
Minister of Morningside, 1868–1873,
Principal of the University of Aberdeen,
1900–1909

Portrait by Swan Watson, F.R.P.S.

1900–1914
Rev. ROBERT H. FISHER, D.D.

Portrait by Edward R. Yerbury, F.R.P.S.

1914–1939
Rev. ANDREW BROWN, D.D.

60

HISTORY OF THE PARISH CHURCH

" Who builds a Church to God, and not to fame,
Will never mark the marble with his name."

POPE, *Of the use of riches.*

SO it was with the douce residenters of Morningside, who took up so heartily in 1837 the " Proposal to build a Church for the Village and surrounding district." There was then no place of worship nearer than St Cuthbert's, to whose Ministers, the Rev. David Dickson, D.D., and the Rev. John Paul, graceful acknowledgment was made in the proposal referred to : " among other labours among us Divine Service has been regularly performed in the School Room of the Village for upwards of twenty years, once a week on the Thursday evenings, and latterly on the Sabbath evenings."

The grant of a site, as indicated earlier, valued then at 200 guineas, was made by Sir John Stuart Forbes, Bart., of Pitsligo and Fettercairn, proprietor of the lands of Greenhill, and the list of subscribers, dated 25th December 1837, was headed by Mr Alexander Falconar of Falcon Hall, followed by his five daughters. Other liberal donors were Sir George Warrender, Bart., of Bruntsfield House ; the Right Hon. Lady Napier and the Trustees of the late Lord Napier, of Merchiston Castle ; the Governors of George Watson's Hospital ; the Managers of the Royal Asylum (which had received its Charter in 1807, and had recently acquired a large part of the adjacent village of Tipperlinn) ; Charles Chalmers (brother of Dr Thomas Chalmers), Headmaster, " and the young gentlemen of Merchiston Academy " ; General Robertson, Canaan Bank ; Sir John Steell, Sculptor-Royal ; Mr George Seton, St Bennet's ; Mr Donald R. M'Gregor of Woodburn, and many other neighbours and well-wishers. The contributions from others beyond the immediate locality, doubtless many of them visitors to the Montpellier of the east of Scotland, as the delightfully restful district was then regarded, included Lady Colquhoun of Luss ; Benjamin Bell, famous surgeon [1] ; and John Abercrombie, the celebrated Edinburgh physician. A grant of £237, 15s. was made from the Church of Scotland Extension Fund of that day, inaugurated both for Edinburgh and Glasgow by the Rev. Thomas Chalmers, D.D., LL.D. (1780–1847), Professor of Divinity in the University of Edinburgh, orator, philosopher, and statesman, one of the most potent Scottish personalities

---

[1] His great-grandson was Joseph Bell, Surgeon to the Royal Infirmary, and prototype of *Sherlock Holmes.*

61

of his time. Morningside was one of the first results of that movement. In 1838 he was pleading for Church Extension before crowded audiences in London.

COMMUNION PLATE 1838
90 ounces. Edinburgh Hall Mark, 1837 (Reign of King William IV.)
Presented by Mr Alexander Falconar of Falcon Hall to " our rural sanctuary "

The boundaries were fixed as " that part of the Parish of St Cuthbert's bounded on the north by the canal, running south in a line to Braidhill to the point where Colinton and St Cuthbert's parishes meet, and then eastwards to the point where the parishes of Liberton and St Cuthbert's meet, then north by the east end of Blackford Hill," to be disjoined from the Parish of St Cuthbert's and erected into a new *quoad sacra* parish to be called the Parish of Morningside. The actual " disjunction " was effected by the Court of Teinds, 20th July 1864, and a Deed of Constitution granted, which was superseded by the " Model Deed of Constitution " of 31st October 1933, with a Congregational Board, following upon the Union with the United Free Church in 1929 (for which the Very Rev. William Mair, D.D.—1830–1920—the great authority on Church Law, had worked so long and earnestly). The previous Union of 1900 had united the Free Church and the United Presbyterian as the United Free Church of Scotland.

OPENING SERVICES

In all, a sum of £2075, 16s. was raised, including the value of the site, and the necessary funds having been thus provided it was unanimously resolved to proceed with the undertaking, " *so as not to leave One Shilling of*

Photo by W. Mair

COLLECTION LADLES, 1839

debt remaining on the Building." [1] The General Assembly having enacted the Constitution on 28th May 1838, the Opening Services were conducted on Sabbath, 29th July 1838, Dr Thomas Chalmers preaching in the forenoon, the collections on that day amounting to £52, 4s. 3¼d., all meticulously engrossed in the Sederunt Book. The newspaper report stated that " there was an overflowing audience and many went away unable to obtain admittance. Dr Chalmers preached with all his accustomed eloquence and power "—from the text, " I have planted, Apollos watered ; but God gave the increase." (1 Cor. iii. 6.)

Already they had opened an account for the building of a Manse ; they had provided a pulpit gown for the Minister at a cost of £6, 17s. 6d.

[1] The Architect was Mr John Henderson. A drawback, or rebate of duty, on wood and glass was obtained, amounting to £120.

(by 1865 the cost of the same item had increased to £16, 7s. 6d.). As early as 1840 a collection was made for providing coals for the poor of the village and places adjacent. The bell, costing £27, 16s. 11d., had come from Whitechapel Foundry. Eighteen pounds of " candles for lighting the church " were required in 1841 (gas lighting was installed in 1852). Electric lighting was introduced in 1903, and renewed in 1931 by the present efficient system, eliminating pendants.

Then came the unsettled period as between Church and State, and the question of parish presentees, which culminated in the Disruption of 1843. The Minister—the Rev. Thomas Addis—seceded along with five hundred others, including those of many of the richest livings in Scotland. It was a staggering blow, and it was recorded in the Minutes that the Trustees and Managers had to take into consideration " the peculiar and unprecedented situation arising from the recent Disruption and Secession from the Church of Scotland " of so many of their members. They were obliged to rescind a decision come to in 1841 regarding the building of a Manse, the sum in hand then amounting to £219, 2s. 3d., which sum was ultimately applied to supplying the resulting deficiency in the usual revenues of the " chapel of ease," as it was called in the legal documents.

If there was pain in leaving the old churches, the loved scenes of former labour, yet the real point of anxiety was the first meeting of the several Free Church congregations on the succeeding Sabbath. Sometimes the meeting was held in the Minister's house, for the most part however, in this memorable summer of 1843, it was in the open air, sometimes in the stackyards of the farms.

ENLARGEMENT AND PROGRESS

Two of the Ministers of Morningside, and one former Assistant, have been Moderator of the General Assembly of the Church of Scotland— Dr John Marshall Lang in 1893, Dr M'Adam Muir in 1910, and Dr George Milligan in 1923. Dr Lang's successor was the Rev. Malcolm C. Taylor, D.D., from Crathie, where he was Chaplain-in-Ordinary to Queen Victoria, and later to King Edward VII. and to King George V. He was inducted to the parish on 27th November 1873, and resigned 3rd October 1879 on his appointment to the Chair of Divinity and Ecclesiastical History at Edinburgh University. Emeritus Professor M. C. Taylor remained a member of the Parish Church till his decease in 1922. Early in 1880 the Rev. Pearson M'Adam Muir was elected, and in 1881 the Manse, in Morningside Park, with its somewhat cloistered seclusion of a high wall and forest trees, was purchased at a cost of £3230.

A period of great activity was now entered upon. During 1883 it was felt that additional church accommodation was required for the parish, and it was considered whether this could be attained by the enlargement

THE MANSE, 52 Morningside Park

of the Parish Church or whether an iron Church should be erected within the extensive boundaries. The latter course was decided on ; a new iron Church was purchased at a cost of £650 and erected near Morningside Toll, at what is now No. 2 Cluny Avenue, opposite the suburban station, which was opened a year later, in 1884. The Rev. George Milligan, B.D.,[1] then Assistant in the Parish Church, was appointed Minister, this being the nucleus of St Matthew's, completed in 1901 at a total cost, including the site, of between £18,000 and £20,000, one of the two daughter Churches of Morningside. The other, St Oswald's, in Montpelier Park, had its origin in the same little iron Church, which was sold to St Mark's congregation in 1890, its name changed later from St Mark's to St Oswald's, and transferred to Bruntsfield. This second daughter Church was built at a cost, including the organ (£800) of £12,736. Both were established in the time of Dr M'Adam Muir, a ministry of great achievement, and both were erected later into independent Parish Churches.

The actual site of the toll-house (page 39) had been considered. This

[1] Later D.D. ; Professor of Biblical Criticism, University of Glasgow ; Moderator of the General Assembly, 1923. Died 25th November 1934.

focal point at the foot of the hill very nearly became a similar one to that at the top of the hill (page 14). The U.P. in the same year (1883) also planted an iron Church (illustrated) (now Braid Church of Scotland) in the

From a Water-colour by E. Michie, A.R.S.A.

IRON CHURCH AT JUNCTION OF BRAID ROAD
AND ROAD TO COMISTON (1883)
(The first Braid Church)

open field, now the Commercial Bank corner. The Free Church in 1889 commenced services in the Hall, Morningside Drive, ultimately building in 1891 at Braid Road and Cluny Drive, now South Morningside Church of Scotland.

MODERN CHURCH FURNISHING

The Pulpit is semi-pentagonal in shape, designed 1931, by Mr LESLIE GRAHAME THOMSON, R.S.A., F.R.I.B.A., and executed in fumed oak by Messrs Scott Morton. Four of the panels, picked out in colour, contain the emblems of the Evangelists—the Angel of St Matthew, the Lion of St Mark, the Ox of St Luke, and the Eagle of St John. A fifth panel contains the Phœnix rising from the flames—the emblem of Resurrection. The fall on the Pulpit bookboard is of the Ark upon the waters and under the rainbow, symbolising God's promise to His people. The Chancel window is a triptych, by an unknown artist, erected 1871. It presents, in nine pictorial panels, an epitome of the life of Our Lord, the central theme

66

Photo by Mr William D. Leask.

PULPIT AND CHANCEL, MORNINGSIDE PARISH CHURCH

THE BAPTISMAL FONT IN CAEN STONE,
AND LECTERN

Presented on the Fiftieth Anniversary, 1888

67

being The Last Supper. The ministers' chairs and kneelers are richly carved with varied floral ornament and with angels holding shields with various ecclesiastical devices. The minister's Communion chair has, in addition, a carved panel of the Pelican in her Piety, *i.e.*, the old legend that a Pelican fed her young with drops of her own blood, and represents self-sacrifice for others, most notably that of our Lord for us on Calvary, and is therefore also emblematical of the Last Supper.

THE ORGAN

Mr HORACE W. BELL, Organist of the Parish Church, has contributed the following note :—

Designed and built in 1921 by Henry Willis & Sons, Ltd., one of the foremost of organ builders, the organ is a fine example of the builder's art. The specification, drawn up by the late Dr Collinson, provides as much tonal variety as is possible in an instrument of its size. In carrying out this specification the builders have combined an excellent balance of tone qualities with a high degree of tonal dignity, the voicing of the reeds being especially fine.

EARLY MUSICAL HISTORY

" On a ten-stringed instrument
upon the psaltery."

PSALM xcii.

Almost immediately after the Rev. John Marshall Lang's appointment in 1868 the Church was enlarged by the addition of an apse and the building of the north and south transepts. It was reseated as it is now : previously there had been no centre passageway. During the nine months occupied by these alterations the Services were held in Merchiston Castle School. On the re-opening in the following year Mr Lang introduced, among other innovations, as they were then regarded, that of requiring the congregation to stand during church praise and to sit or kneel during prayers. The young minister (he was thirty-four) had great faith in the importance of good music in the prosperity of a church, and it was as a result of the interest and encouragement given to the Choir by Mr and Mrs Lang, their regular attendance at the practices, and their desire to improve the congregational singing that a Choral Society was formed in 1869. It was an immediate success, and had a membership of over eighty. The voluntary membership of the Choir was then so large that it was practicable for a time to form three choirs, who took their places in the church in alternate months. During the six years of Dr Lang's ministry popular recitals were given of works by Handel, Haydn, Mendelssohn, and other great composers, with the accompaniment of a harmonium, which, however, was *never played on Sundays :* instrumental music was not introduced till 1875. The church was invariably crowded at these week-day concerts, which were a centre of musical culture for a larger public than that of the then limited Morningside area, and the proceeds went a long way, as was intended, towards completing the transformed and beautiful Sanctuary.

The Organ, as has been indicated, was installed in 1875. It cost £700, and did duty for forty-six years. It was replaced in 1921 by the present organ, and it is insured for £4000. The first Organist and Choirmaster was William Jackson, *Te Deum* Jackson, from the Conservatoire, Stuttgart. He was followed by Herr Franz Walter, a native of Basle, Switzerland, a highly skilled and brilliant executant. Both of these gifted musicians died young ; and in the Jubilee Year, 1888—when the apse was transformed into a Chancel and the organ removed from the gallery, where it faced the pulpit, to its present position—W. H. Hopkinson became Organist. He initiated another era of great musical activity for the Choir. They had joint vocal and instrumental recitals, and named themselves the " Philharmonic," as was the order of the day. At one of their concerts of popular pieces, held in the Athenæum (page 14), it was crowded to the door, the receipts, with a repeat performance, amounting to over £40.

ST MATTHEW'S

The origin of this stately edifice dates, as has been indicated, from a Congregational Meeting held in the Parish Church in 1883. The architect was the late Hippolyte J. Blanc, R.S.A., F.R.I.B.A. (1844–1917). Its Chancel is regarded as one of the most chaste and ornate specimens of such artistic work in the country. The Nave is 80 ft. long by 42 ft. wide and proportionately lofty. The stained glass in the East (Chancel) window and that in the great West window are among the finest in Edinburgh and are held in great affection.

A notable addition in the North transept fittingly commemorates the late Rev. Frank Hale Martin, B.D., who was Minister here for twenty-nine years (1912–41), a man greatly beloved for his gracious, saintly life and example, who died on 5th May 1941, at sixty-nine years. It takes the form of a large upright mural panel of Pericot marble, 6 ft. by 3 ft., and was dedicated on 4th May 1947 by the Very Rev. Professor Daniel Lamont, D.D., and the Rev. R. C. M. Mathers, M.A., Minister of the Parish. The memorial was designed and executed by Mr C. d'O Pilkington Jackson, sculptor, and consists of a Celtic cross based on that of St Martin's at Iona, surrounded by a carved and ornamental framework, all embellished in gold.

69

HISTORIC MORNINGSIDE :

NORTH MORNINGSIDE CHURCH

The following is contributed by Mr ROBERT W. COCKBURN, W.S., J.P., Session Clerk :—

The congregation was formed in 1861 out of a small band of members who met in a classroom of Merchiston Castle School. They built a church on the northern corner of Chamberlain Road, opposite to the present site, which became later the property of Morningside Congregational Church and was replaced by their fine building (page 14). The beginnings were slow and difficult until the Rev. Alexander Mair (afterwards Dr) became Minister in 1873. The present church was opened in 1881. The style of architecture is Norman, as practised in Scotland during the twelfth century, and it is the only example in Edinburgh of Norman art as applied to a modern ecclesiastical structure : the bell tower rises to a height of 110 ft. The church is seated for over one thousand worshippers.

Three noble stained-glass windows in the eastern clerestory were dedicated in 1920 as a remembrance of the epic years, 1914–19. Three others in the western clerestory are memorials to former ministers : that to Dr Mair was intended to suggest The Pastor and his active ministry here of twenty-nine years. He was the last Moderator of the United Presbyterian body at the time of its Union with the Free Church. He died in 1911, but eight years earlier, the membership having reached eight hundred, the Rev. D. W. Forrest, D.D. had become his colleague. The second window recalls Dr Forrest as The Teacher. He was one of the leading theologians of his time, and two of his books, *The Christ of History and of Experience* and *The Authority of Christ*, had a very wide circulation. Dr Forrest brought to the work of the ministry in North Morningside, ripe scholarship, wide culture, and deep spiritual insight. He was appointed Professor of Systematic Theology and Apologetics in the Glasgow College. The third of these windows, to the Rev. James G. Goold, M.A., by Misses Chilton and Kemp, 1925, emphasises The Preacher. His distinguished ministry here was succeeded by that of the Rev. D. H. Hislop, M.A., who resigned his charge at the end of 1934 on account of ill health. A stained glass window to his memory, by the late John Duncan, R.S.A., was placed in the western aisle. A stained glass window in three lights, dedicated in 1930, commemorates the founders, thirty-seven in number, of the congregation in 1861.

The Rev. James S. Stewart, B.D., from Beechgrove, Aberdeen, was appointed in May 1935. The membership had remained round eight hundred since the late nineties of last century, but Mr Stewart's reputation as a great evangelical scholar and preacher soon attracted large numbers to the membership. On receiving the degree of D.D. from the University of St Andrews in 1945, he was described by the promotor as " one of the great preachers of the generation." The membership had reached over 1,750 when he resigned his charge as at the end of 1946 on appointment to the Chair of New Testament Literature, Language, and Theology in Edinburgh University (New College).

Dr Stewart has made notable contributions to theological and religious literature and his books are as well known in the United States and in the Colonies as in this country. Chief among these are his study of *St Paul, a Man in Christ*, which has run into many editions, and his Warrack lectures on preaching, *Heralds of God*, recently published. He is succeeded by Rev. Roderick Bethune, M.A., also from Beechgrove, Aberdeen.

GREENBANK CHURCH

The following is contributed by Mr DUNCAN MACLENNAN, S.S.C., Session-Clerk :—

Within the later decades of last century, South Morningside had become a populous suburb, and by the end of the century it had already been well provided with places of worship—in Braid Church, by the United Presbyterian Church of Scotland ; St Matthew's, by the Church of Scotland ; and South Morningside Church, by the Free Church of Scotland.

The need that would eventually arise for a church still farther south than any of these—in the direction of Greenbank and the Braid Hills—had also then been foreseen, and with the sanction of the Presbytery of the United Presbyterian Church a Hall was built on part of a site about half a mile southwards from Morningside Station opposite what is now the entrance to Braidburn Valley Park. With a view to the formation of a congregation there, the Hall was opened for public worship on Sunday, 13th May 1900, and on 16th June of that year thirty-five certified members were declared to be a congregation of the United Presbyterian Church, being then enrolled by the Presbytery as the congregation of Greenbank with two Elders from the Braid Church to form the nucleus of a Kirk Session.

The Union of the United Presbyterian Church and the Free Church, constituting the United Free Church of Scotland, took place in October 1900, and about a year later Greenbank congregation was authorised by the Presbytery of the united body to call a Minister. The Rev. Norman Fraser, B.D., was inducted on 20th February 1902, a man of scholarly attainments and an interesting preacher, who ministered to the congregation for about eleven years increasing the membership to about 300.

Mr Fraser's successor was the Rev. T. Ratcliffe Barnett of St Andrew's Church, Bo'ness, who was inducted on 21st January 1914. During the whole period of Mr Fraser's ministry the congregation continued to worship in the commodious and comfortable Hall, but with the settlement of a new Minister the time seemed to be ripe to set about making plans for the building of the Church on the part of the site adjoining the Hall, which had been left vacant for the purpose. Hardly, however, had the matter been raised when there came the declaration of the first World War, in August 1914, followed some time later by Dr Barnett's absence on service with the troops. The years immediately succeeding the war were naturally inappropriate for the launching of a church building scheme, but by 1925 the project was well on the way and was then pursued with such zeal and energy that the foundation stone of the new church was laid on 24th April 1926, and the completed church opened and dedicated for public worship on 8th October 1927. The interior is on simple but dignified lines, accommodating about 600 people, and, with its three memorial stained-glass windows adding their rich note of colour, it forms an attractive place of worship. Including the value of furnishings given by members and friends (but not the windows) the total cost involved was about £19,000, which under Dr Barnett's enthusiastic leadership was almost entirely contributed before the opening date. The advantages of a well-equipped church soon began to be evident, and Dr Barnett—he had been awarded the degree of Doctor of Philosophy by the University of Edinburgh in 1925—had the satisfaction of seeing the congregation grow and prosper under his watchful ministry. He thought it best, however, to make way for a younger man while the congregational activities were still in full working order, and he resigned at the end of 1938, having then completed a ministry of almost exactly twenty-five years, and leaving a vigorous and well-knit congregation with a Communion Roll of over 800 members.

Greenbank Church was always the first charge on Dr Barnett's time, but his name became widely known throughout Scotland and farther afield as a traveller who could record with interest and distinction what he observed in well-remembered scenes and among Scottish folk. His holidays, usually spent in tramps among the mountains and the moors of Scotland, or by her rivers of romance, provided him with rich material for a succession of books the very titles of which almost carry the breath of the wind on the heath or the sound of languid breakers on lone Atlantic shores. Such are *The Road to Rannoch and the Summer Isles*, *The Land of Lochiel and the Magic West*, *The Land of Lorne and the Isles of Rest*, *Scottish Pilgrimage in the Land of Lost Content*, *The Winds of Dawn*, *Autumns in Skye, Ross, and Sutherland*, which has recently been reprinted. Other fascinating books are *Highland Harvest* and *Border Byways and Lothian Lore*. In another vein are *Fairshiels : Memories of a Lammermoor Parish*, an affectionate tribute to the people of his first charge of Fala and Blackshiels, alongside of which may be mentioned as belonging to the period of Fairshiels, *The Finest Baby in the World*, *The Blessed Ministry of Childhood*, and *The Dame of the Fine Green Kirtle*. At intervals too, there came *Reminiscences of Old Scots Folk*, *The Makers of the Scottish Kirk*, *Margaret of Scotland, Queen and Saint*, and *The Story of the Covenant*, while in his later years he put the notes of a visit to Palestine and the Middle East into most readable form in a small volume entitled *The Cradle of Christianity*.

Dr Barnett died on 20th February 1946, having survived the date of his retirement by a period of just over seven years.

The present Minister of Greenbank Church of Scotland is the Rev. David H. C. Read, B.D. Called from Coldstream only a month or two before the outbreak of the second World War, Mr Read was not inducted until after the War was declared. By the time of his induction, on 8th October 1939, he had been mobilised as a Chaplain to the Forces, and being stationed in the south of England he was prevented from taking up his ministry at Greenbank, preaching there only on three occasions when on short leave before proceeding overseas. Soon after reaching France he was captured at St Valery (in June 1940) and was held a prisoner of war in Germany until April 1945, returning eventually to Greenbank at the end of September of that year, almost exactly six years after his induction. Since that time he has been ministering to an ever-growing congregation numbering now about 1000 members, a figure which in its implications surely reflects great credit on the faith and foresight of the pioneering thirty-five of the year 1900.

Not only, however, is Mr Read the active Minister of a large and devoted congregation, but through the radio he is a frequent and welcome interpreter of the Christian message to multitudes of eager listeners scattered over the whole country, to whom Greenbank Church is now a familiar name. He, too, has his own gift of writing, and, in addition to articles contributed to various periodicals, he has already to his credit such vital volumes as *The Spirit of Life* and *Prisoners' Quest*. He had the distinction of preaching before the King and Queen at Crathie Kirk, Deeside, on Sabbath, 24th August 1947, also on a previous occasion in 1938.

CHRIST CHURCH

The following notes are contributed by Mr HAROLD SKELTON :—

In 1874 about one hundred and fifty Episcopalians worshipped weekly on Sundays in the Drill-Hall of Merchiston Castle School.[1] At that time

[1] Nursery of young congregations (pages 70 and 73).

there was no church for members of that faith between Tollcross and Roslin. It was decided in 1875 to build a church, with Mr Hippolyte J. Blanc (page 69) as architect, and the Nave was completed and opened for worship on Whitsunday, 4th June 1876. Miss Falconar of Falcon Hall (page 29) defrayed the cost of the Chancel, Tower, and Spire. She died in 1887 in her ninetieth year. The church was dedicated by Bishop Cotterill of Edinburgh on Whitsunday, 1878.

The style of the structure is French Gothic of the thirteenth century, wide nave and quasi-transepts, roofs open to the ridge. The richly appointed memorial Chancel ends in a polygonal apse with processional aisle, the roof groined in wood, the walls having rich diapering carved in stone : the stained glass in the long windows of the apsidal clerestory were the work of James Ballantyne & Sons, Edinburgh. The children's window of stained glass (also by Ballantyne) was completed in 1887. Two windows unveiled in 1893 (Ballantyne & Gardner) are in memory of the Rev. F. S. Belcombe, first Rector of Christ Church. A central figure in another window is that of St Luke, in memory of Dr Bruce A. Bremner, one of the original members, gifted by members of his family. The Jubilee window in the west wall was designed and executed by Captain A. E. Borthwick, R.S.A., P.R.S.W., a member of the congregation.

ST PETER'S, Falcon Avenue

Built on Falcon Hall estate in 1906, to the designs of the late Sir Robert Lorimer, A.R.A., LL.D. (1864–1929), architect of the Thistle Chapel, St Giles', and of the Shrine, Edinburgh Castle, this beautiful little sanctuary contains many notable works of ecclesiastical art, all by famous artists. Twelve devotional paintings by the late John Duncan, R.S.A., R.S.W., represent progressively " The Stations of the Cross." The altarpiece is by Sir Frank Brangwyn, R.A., LL.D., and the six fine stained-glass windows are by Meredith Williams. Other valuable paintings include one, " The Flight into Egypt," and there is a bronze statue of St Peter, seated. The church accommodates four hundred. The home of the Archbishop of St Andrews and Edinburgh, the Most Reverend Andrew J. M'Donald, O.S.B.,[1] is at St Bennet's, 42 Greenhill Gardens, nearby.

[1] Order of Saint Benedict.

ECCLESIASTICAL MORNINGSIDE

THE OLD SCHOOLHOUSE, 1823
Illustrated on page 26

As has been noted, the village schoolhouse was in 1838 the only place of worship of the rural community. In addition to the visiting ministers there named, Dr Thomas Chalmers often preached in it. It thus preceded by about twenty years his " Church on the Hill," as he loved to call it. It was the Hall of the Parish Church opposite, for many years after its school days closed and has since then been a Mission station. Recently it has been purchased on behalf of the active little congregation known as the Brethren, who hold services and church activities there, by one of their number. It is likely now to undertake responsibility for a medical missionary in the Belgian Congo.

Theirs is a beautiful simple service of earnest prayer and hearty praise, without ritual, unaccompanied and without choir. They acknowledge no special distinction as between clergy and laity : the first sect formed on these lines was in 1830 as the Society of Believers. The hymns were selected in London for " The little Flock " in 1856 and re-edited in 1881 and 1903. Practically any brother may share in the conduct of the service, excepting only those " not gifted with utterance." Communion is dispensed at every Sabbath morning service and there is a hand-shake and a welcome to visitors at the close of every service.

ARCHBISHOP AND MODERATOR

Reprinted, by permission, from THE PROCEEDINGS of the GENERAL ASSEMBLY for 1935
page 400

The Moderator of that year was the Very Rev. MARSHALL B. LANG, T.D., D.D., F.S.A.(Scot.), author of *The Seven Ages of an East Lothian Parish*, and Minister successively of Meldrum, Aberdeenshire ; St John's (Cross) Parish, Dundee ; and Whittingehame, East Lothian. The Lord High Commissioner was H.R.H. The late DUKE of KENT, K.G.

" The late Dr COSMO GORDON LANG, brother of the Moderator, was seated in the Commissioner's gallery. ' It was with gratitude and joy,' said Professor Lamont, ' that they had with them in the House the head of their great sister Communion, the Archbishop of Canterbury.'

" The Moderator, in welcoming him, said, ' Your Grace ' (the remainder of the sentence was drowned in applause and laughter). ' It is a very singular pleasure,' he continued, ' to welcome you to the floor of the Assembly, not only as one I have been familiar with in past years (renewed laughter), but as representing the great sister Communion of England.' (Applause.)

" The venerable Archbishop said that he had not come prepared with any address worthy of the Assembly, or of its traditions. ' I must content myself,' he continued, ' in the fewest possible words, in saying with what satisfaction I find that the choice of Moderator this year has rested upon one of whom at least I can say that he belongs to a highly respectable family, and that he has maintained its traditions of respectability, orthodoxy, and fidelity to the Church of his fathers, more successfully than an elder brother. (Laughter.) With all my heart I pray that God's blessing may continually rest upon the Church of my fathers.' (Loud applause.)

" The Moderator expressed the gratitude of the Assembly to the Archbishop for the words he had spoken and for the blessing he had given to them as fathers and brethren of the Church of Scotland."

The very Rev. PRINCIPAL JOHN MARSHALL LANG, C.V.O., D.D., LL.D., father of the two eminent Divines, was Moderator of the General Assembly in 1893. During his reign of six years at Morningside, in addition to the enlargement of the Church, noted on page 68, seven of the ten Memorial stained-glass windows were gifted and dedicated.

A GLIMPSE OF THE EIGHTEEN-HUNDREDS
by
WILLIAM MAIR

In 1800 the population of Edinburgh, including Leith, was 82,000, Mr David Robertson, LL.B., former Town Clerk, has recorded, and he adds that " it was the intellectual centre of the Kingdom rather than London." It was the heyday of *The Edinburgh Review* (1802-1929). Only ten years previously, in 1789, Robert Burns was wont to take his favourite walk southwards to " the furzy hills of Braid," then, as now in the spring in all the golden glory of gorse and whin, with his friend, Professor Dugald Stewart, F.R.S., the philosopher. They had met in Ayrshire, where the latter's father had a country place, at Catrine. It was a bright, brief interlude in a life that saw more shadow than sunshine, the poet's sojourn among the literary and the learned of the Capital. He wrote in his *Address to Edinburgh* [1] :—

> " There learning, with his eagle eyes,
>   seeks Science in her coy abode."

From the Braids he would look down on Duddingston, crowned with the Castle of Craigmillar, and on " the sleepy hollow of Morningside."

In 1837 Queen Victoria had just succeeded " Uncle William," and had reached her eighteenth birthday. She was Queen indeed, almost to her surprise—" poor stupid me," she wrote in her *Journal*. Penny Postage had been realised, one of the many centenaries celebrated in 1940 ; the era of railways had just been inaugurated ; David Octavius Hill, R.S.A., was making the first photographs, calotypes, at his studio on the Calton Hill

[1] The MS. is in the Library of Edinburgh University.

Photo by Mr Robert Lawson.

THE KIRK ON THE HILL
North and South Transepts added 1869

steps. These artistic achievements he built up into the colossal painting (57 sq. ft.,—11½ ft. by 5 ft.) of the signing of the " Act of Separation and Deed of Demission " in 1843, containing 500 portraits, to be seen in the stately Presbytery Hall of the Free Church on the Mound. The minister of the neighbouring 800-year old Duddingston Kirk, the Rev. John Thomson (1778–1840), was preaching and painting with marked success in both of these spheres, especially the latter. It is said that for ten years, from 1820 to 1830, his landscapes brought him £1800 a year, a considerable amount of which went out in benevolence. He had three large canvases in the Scottish Academy of 1838. In that year the Academy, founded 1826, received its Royal Charter, becoming R.S.A. The sedan chair had not gone quite out of vogue for conveying ladies to evening parties and the theatre. It cost two shillings by sedan chair between Edinburgh and Leith. There was a duty of one penny on every copy of *The Scotsman*, then published only twice a week, on Wednesday and Saturday, at fourpence-halfpenny, plus tax. On the repeal of the tax in 1855 *The Scotsman* became a daily at a penny. It described the sudden passing of Dr Thomas Chalmers (30th May 1847, at 67) as that of " perhaps the greatest, certainly the best beloved, Scotsman of the present generation." The smithy beside the Old Schoolhouse on Morningside Road was the first stop from the city boundary for the many carriers entering the city with country produce from Biggar and the south. Here would halt James Noble, the Howgate carrier, and Ailie, " pale, serious, delicate, sweet "—and Rab [1] on the way to Syme's own hospital at Old Minto House, where Dr John Brown was house surgeon. R.L.S. said that Brown

> " . . . didna fash himsel' to think—
> Ye stapped yer pen into the ink,
> And there was *Rab*."

[1] *Rab and his Friends* (1859), by John Brown, M.D. (1810–82).

INDEX

HISTORIC MORNINGSIDE :

ECCLESIASTICAL MORNINGSIDE
and some " Annals of the Parish "

PHOTOGRAPHIC VIEW INDICATOR ON BRAID HILLS, EDINBURGH

Reproduction on one-third scale

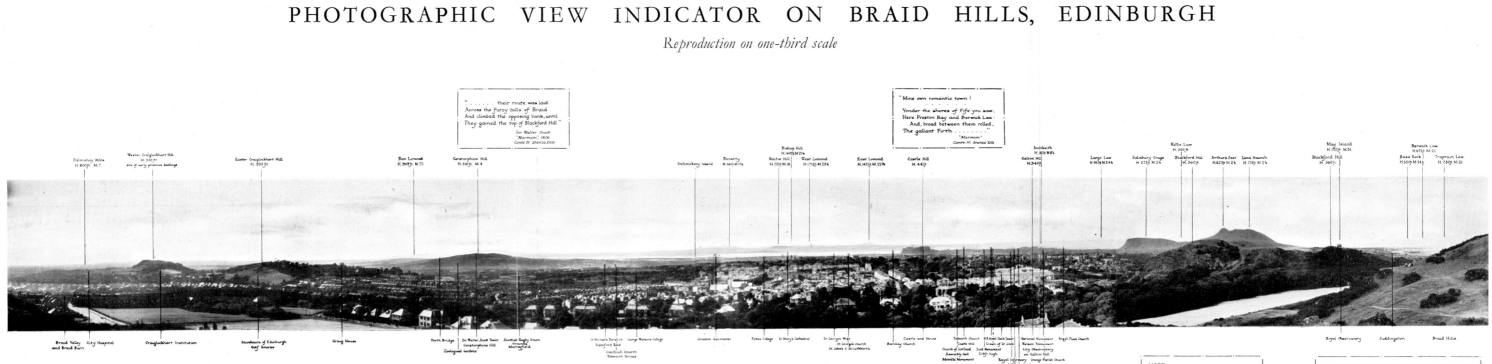

" . . . . . . their route was laid
Across the furzy hills of Braid,
And climbed the opposing bank, until
They gained the top of Blackford Hill."
Sir Walter Scott
"Marmion", 1806
Canto IV. Stanza XXIII

" Mine own romantic town !
. . . .
Yonder the shores of Fife you saw,
Here Preston Bay and Berwick Law :
And, broad between them rolled,
The gallant Firth . . . . "
"Marmion"
Canto IV. Stanza XXX

NOTE :
True North and South line passes 100 yards
E. of St Cuthbert's Parish Church.

The GEOGRAPHICAL (Disc) INDICATOR, also from this view point,
and the ELEVATIONS above sea level, and DISTANCES
by JOHN MATHIESON, F.R.S.E., F.R.S.G.S., 1936.